SMUGGLED

Ruth Balint is an associate professor of history at the University of New South Wales. She teaches and writes about forced migration, family and refugees in the twentieth century. Her family were refugees from Europe before and after the Second World War. Her latest book, *Destination Elsewhere: Displaced Persons and their Quest to Leave Europe after 1945*, is published by Cornell University Press.

Julie Kalman is an associate professor of history at Monash University. She writes about the history of French Jews, after the French Revolution and also following the Second World War. She is the child of migrants from Europe, and she has researched and published on topics related to her own history, including the history of migration to Australia, and the Eurovision Song Contest.

'*Smuggled* is a pioneering work in Australian immigration history. The history of illegal journeys is a topic rarely discussed let alone researched in any depth. The powerful stories recounted in this compelling book about people smuggling write a new chapter in the history of displacement through the extraordinary experiences of courage, survival, and resilience. It is inspiring research which transforms our understanding of the history of migration to Australia through an evocative new lens.'

PROFESSOR JOY DAMOUSI, AUSTRALIAN CATHOLIC UNIVERSITY

'*Smuggled* is an enthralling book. Each chapter is a short story of a separate and unique journey to safety; dangerous, desperate and daring. Each story adds to our understanding of a smuggler as a person who is often so much more than an unscrupulous criminal. They are frequently skilled facilitators, brave guides and caring escorts. They range from diplomats to simple villagers. It may suit some politicians to colour smugglers as money hungry crooks, but without their help, the refugees in this book, and most refugees in general, would never have made it to Australia to build worthwhile lives. *Smuggled* is a new, important way to tell our migration history, and is a fascinating read.'

ANDREW AND RENATA KALDOR, KALDOR CENTRE FOR INTERNATIONAL REFUGEE LAW, UNIVERSITY OF NEW SOUTH WALES

'A combination of engaging stories and astute analysis, *Smuggled* is a timely corrective to the simplistic portrayal of people smugglers as evil scum. Some smugglers may be heroes and some may be villains, but to blame them for the suffering of refugees is to deflect from more important concerns, including the oppression that drives people from their homes and the border controls that force them onto dangerous routes.'

PETER MARES, THE CRANLANA CENTRE FOR ETHICAL LEADERSHIP

SMUGGLED

AN ILLEGAL HISTORY OF JOURNEYS TO AUSTRALIA

Ruth Balint and Julie Kalman

NEWSOUTH

A NewSouth book

Published by
NewSouth Publishing
University of New South Wales Press Ltd
University of New South Wales
Sydney NSW 2052
AUSTRALIA
newsouthpublishing.com

© Ruth Balint and Julie Kalman 2021
First published 2021

10 9 8 7 6 5 4 3 2 1

A catalogue record for this book is available from the National Library of Australia

ISBN: 9781742236896 (paperback)
         9781742245140 (ebook)
         9781742249667 (ePDF)

Design Josephine Pajor-Markus
Cover design Susanne Geppert
Cover artwork The little fish was the riverboat (From the Horse's Mouth), 2019
    Phuong Ngo

UNSW
SYDNEY

CONTENTS

INTRODUCTION: PEOPLE SMUGGLING AND AUSTRALIAN MIGRATION HISTORY

Ruth Balint and Julie Kalman

In the past two decades, the world's media has been awash with images of sinking boats crammed with desperate people, bodies washed up on beaches or dead in the backs of lorries, and of children behind barbed wire. Nowadays, the refugee has become synonymous with both illegality and victimhood in the public imagination, closely associated with irregular border crossings and crooks, even as they are simultaneously imagined as victims. It is within this recent context that the term 'people smuggler' has emerged to encapsulate the criminality of refugee flight. It evokes a clandestine world of unscrupulous individuals connected to mafia networks, preying on vulnerable people and undermining proper, orderly and humanitarian migration processes. We might argue that the 'evil' people smuggler has become the bogeyman of the Western world, rivalled only by terrorists and paedophiles, and demonising people smugglers is something of a sport among politicians. 'People smugglers are engaged in the world's most evil trade and they should all rot in jail because they represent the absolute scum of the earth,' thundered Prime Minister Kevin Rudd in 2009, in just one notable example.[1]

But people smuggling is not as new a phenomenon as might be suggested by the language of crisis usually employed by our politicians and the media. The practice is far older and more complex than discussions of organised crime might suggest. For as long as states, kingdoms and empires have sought ways to manage the movement of people, people have sought ways to circumvent borders and bypass travel restrictions, and smugglers have been there to help. Mario Kaiser suggests we could go as far back as Moses leading thousands of Jewish slaves out of Egypt, to find the first people smuggler.[2] A little less far back in history, during the French Revolution, slaves were smuggled out of French-controlled Saint-Domingue (today's Haiti) to British Jamaica. In the late nineteenth century, smugglers took Chinese aliens across the Mexican and Canadian borders into the United States. Their methods were later mimicked in the 1920s, by smugglers taking Jews from Eastern Europe into America. These smugglers were operating in contravention of America's new immigration quota restrictions. 'The gates did not simply close,' writes Libby Garland.[3] Instead, a whole underground industry in illegal Jewish immigration, assisted by a vast network of international smugglers in ports and cities across Eastern Europe, Asia and the Americas, functioned to assist Jews escaping worsening economic conditions, political upheaval and anti-Semitic violence in Eastern Europe, Russia and then the Soviet Union.

In *Smuggled: An illegal history of journeys to Australia* we tell the fascinating story of people smuggling in Australia's migrant history, from the Second World War through to the present. This is a new way of telling Australia's immigration history. We show that many who belonged to migrant groups classified by the government of the day as undesirable and unwanted have been helped or smuggled, at some point in their journey, through gates that were officially closed. These stories have not yet made it into the classical narratives of migration, partly because we haven't tended to see illegality as part of this history. Ironically, perhaps, given that immigration nowadays is mostly defined in criminal and warlike terms, in need of closer monitoring, tracking, regulation and securitisation on an entirely new scale.[4] At the same time, our national map has been redrawn in the same language of illegal immigration, with front entry points and back doors, 'arcs of instability' and uninhabited, vulnerable, coastlines. The essays and stories we bring together here remind us that 'illegalised travellers' are part of our immigration history, and that our perspective towards them is shaped by where we sit in time and place.[5]

The official appearance of the 'people smuggler' in Australia dates to the boat crossings that began with small numbers in the late 1990s, and peaked in the early 2000s, reviving historic fears of invasion from our near maritime north. Fear of invasion is a recurring Australian theme. At the beginning of the twentieth century such fears were embodied in the term 'yellow peril'. Settler Australians imagined themselves to be in danger of being swamped by uncontrollable numbers of Asian hordes to our north. At the beginning of the twenty-first century, it was common to read hyperbolic oceanic headlines of the tides, floods, tsunamis and tidal waves of refugees, bearing down on Australia's fragile coastline. These accompanied images of rotting ferries capsizing under the strain of dangerously heavy loads of exhausted passengers sailing across the Timor Sea between Indonesia and Australia. 'Stopping the boats' quickly became the war cry of successive governments, particularly in the wake of the 'Tampa Affair' of 2001, in which one of the biggest container ships in the world became the unlikely carrier for 433 asylum seekers saved from their sinking wooden boat, the *Palapa*. The *Tampa* was forbidden by the Howard Government to land its human cargo on Christmas Island, thus kicking off the infamous 'Pacific Solution' of offshore detention on the island nation of Nauru and the Papua New Guinean island of Manus.

Such crises of sovereignty helpfully offered otherwise struggling leaders a way to promote a strong-armed image of themselves, as men with the necessary muscle to defend a fearful nation's borders.

It was in this time that blame also shifted onto the people smuggler as the main cause of refugee drownings, in keeping with a shift in official rhetoric from a focus on security and border protection to a focus on 'stopping the deaths at sea'. Border protection policies have remained largely the same and, if anything, have become more draconian. As former diplomat and refugee advocate Tony Kevin has written, the tightening of Australia's border protection, with a raft of policies including excising certain islands and reefs from Australia's migration zone or turning boats back, did not stop refugees fleeing war, persecution or disaster, but only served to make journeys more deadly.[6] The notion that the illegalisation of unauthorised human movement would lead people to simply stay put in transit countries like Indonesia or Malaysia or somewhere else, where settlement isn't possible and the only option is to join the 'queue' is folly, but it has continued to drive policy. Instead, the people smuggler has become a convenient distraction from the complex push factors that compel people to leave their homes.

Ali Al Jenabi, one of Australia's more well known people smugglers, tried to imagine this queue that he first heard about in an Australian courtroom. 'What do they think? That when the secret police are shooting at you, you run down the street yelling, "Where's the queue? Where's the queue?"' An Iraqi man who had endured imprisonment in Abu Ghraib under Saddam Hussein's regime, he eventually made it to Indonesia. Here, he began to earn money smuggling people to Ashmore Reef, seven boats in all, so that he could bring his own family to safety. There was no UN office in Iraq, he noted, and the nearest one was two countries away in Pakistan. 'Anyway the belief that there are orderly queues where asylum seekers line up and wait their turn is extraordinary,' he explains. 'Millions of people drift into shambolic UN camps all over the world, and only about two percent are ever settled. For some it takes a few years, for others decades, with many eventually giving up on the UN and finding a smuggler to take them on a boat'.[7] This was reiterated by Dawood Amiri, a refugee who turned to assisting people smugglers in Indonesia in order to help his fellow Hazaras and himself get money to get on a boat to Australia. He described his experience of the UNHCR process of getting formal recognition as a refugee as a 'slow process, choked with red tape'. Jakarta and Bogor, he wrote, 'were full of Afghan, Pakistani, Iranian, Iraqi, and Sri Lankan asylum seekers', most of whom, in his experience, 'were willing to embrace the risk of death by taking to the boats, instead of succumbing to a day-by-day purgatory'.[8]

Australia's fear and loathing of the people smuggler is shared by wealthy countries worldwide, personified by the 'coyotes' that operate between Mexico and the United States, or the Romanian gangsters, 'men in their thirties and forties with Ray-Ban sunglasses, wearing pleated pants and tight nylon shirts'. This is the classic image of the smuggler, men who look like pimps or gypsy kings, 'who carry cell-phones on their belts like pistols'.[9] To this can be added, most recently, the unscrupulous men who patrol Turkish beaches, offering passage across the Mediterranean to the hundreds of thousands of people from Africa and the Middle East, who have gathered there. Writing in 2001, just after the September 11 attacks in New York, Mario Kaiser noted that there were at least four million people who were putting their entire savings in the hands of smugglers as nation states moved to tighten their borders. People smuggling had become the 'fastest-growing area of organised crime', he wrote, 'nearly as profitable as illegal drugs'.[10] It had become its own economy, global and transnational in its reach and networks. Since then, as refugee numbers have swelled to their biggest since the Second World War, the United Nations Office on Drugs and Crime (UNODC) estimates that in 2016 alone, 2.5 million migrants were smuggled for an economic return of US$5.5–7 billion, a staggering amount of money equivalent to what America or the EU spent during the same period on humanitarian aid.[11]

The motivations behind people smuggling are varied and complex. Many who have helped a person undertake an illegal crossing might not recognise themselves as people smugglers. This is borne out by the 2018 UNODC report on smuggling migrants, which noted that as a general pattern, 'smaller-scale smugglers are either ethnically linked to the territories where they operate, or they share ethnic or linguistic ties with the migrants they smuggle'. Anh Do, one of Australia's most loved comedians and media personalities, wrote of his family's investment in their refugee journey after the Vietnam War:

> My extended family pooled all their money, called in favours
> with friends and relatives and sold everything they had – every
> possession – just to buy a boat. Getting your hands on a boat
> was an extremely risky business. They were only available on
> the black market and anyone caught trying to buy one could be
> jailed or killed. After a couple of false starts they finally managed
> to buy a vessel.[12]

Jenabi's decision to smuggle refugees out of Indonesia to Australia, however, had a mix of reasons. 'I am fast becoming part of an underworld of liars and cheats, and the pressure to bring my family out of Iran is increasing.' There was adrenaline in the prospect that he might have his own 'personal victory over Saddam', as much as there was need for cash to help his own family to escape. He admits that he needed the money, he couldn't pretend otherwise. 'However, the fact that they are the means by which I can get my family to safety does not detract from my desires to protect them.' That Jenabi was eventually caught by Australian Federal Police in Thailand, after he had brought 500 people safely to Australia, was unusual. Indonesian fishermen are usually the ones who have done time for the crime of people smuggling in Australian jails. These are the equivalent of

Europe's foot soldiers, paid to take clients across a border and face arrest by border guards. Often, Indonesian boat crews are willing to take the risk of being caught and jailed in Australia on mandatory minimum five-year terms, because whatever money they earn is more than what subsistence fishing or farming brings on the small islands of southeast Indonesia, from where most Indonesian people smuggling crews live and work.

What Jenabi's story also shows is that, contrary to popular assumptions about asylum seekers as passive participants in journeys or routes not of their own making, many are actively involved in decisions about smugglers, routes and destinations. In his own firsthand account, Amiri also upended the usual classification of people smugglers as criminals feeding off the naivety and desperation of asylum seekers. 'Honestly', he writes, 'the people who help asylum-seekers the most are people-smugglers. And these asylum-seekers want to be smuggled.'[13] All of the people whose stories feature in this book were willing participants in illegality. Sometimes, of course, illegality can mean breaking the law to save one's life in a world where that law has turned the basic moral code upside down, such as, for example, the perverse universe of Nazism. Often, what was illegal at one point in the journey was legal at another. These factors – in particular, their agency in the process – differentiate them from trafficked people. Smuggling and trafficking are often used interchangeably as terms, but they describe quite different situations. Vulnerable people have been trafficked throughout history, and, indeed, they continue to be so, tricked or forced into situations of full or semi-slavery.

Khalid Koser and Marie McAuliffe note that with the limited research available, it is clear that migrants exercise agency in choosing smugglers, often for specific destinations of their own choosing. This is particularly so in the Australian context: because of its geographical isolation from other potential refugee settlement countries, people have to actively seek to come here and often have to invest more money and time. In Europe, chance might play a role, as the options are more varied, as much as cost, available routes and distance or terrain. These kinds of factors don't usually apply to Australia. In coming to Australia, people have often made long and relatively expensive journeys from their origin countries, transiting through other countries like Indonesia, where they might have remained in legal limbo for some time. 'The choice of Australia for most unauthorised maritime arrivals appears to be deliberate.'[14]

The experience of these journeys and the smugglers who facilitate them are rarely discussed or known about. This was brought home to an Australian audience in 2011, when much-loved sports commentator and 'soccer king' Les Murray took a filmmaker with him to document his journey back to Hungary, the country he had fled as a boy during the 1956 Revolution. Murray was looking for the man who had helped smuggle him and his family across the border to Austria, a man he knew as Gyula, whom he wanted to find and thank. For Murray, it was the volatile rhetoric around people smuggling that had precipitated his search. Eventually he located the man's family, but Gyula had died three years earlier. At the end of the documentary, Murray sat with Gyula's grandson sharing stories and photos over a beer. 'I am proud of him,' the grandson told Murray upon learning of his grandfather's illicit activities for the first time.

It is true that the people smuggling landscape has changed since Murray made his journey or Anh Do made his. But there is also plenty of evidence to show that not all people smugglers are cut from the same cloth. Accounts such as these, including by smugglers themselves, demystify the shady underworld image that has obscured the industry from view. The stories we tell in this book, which traverse Australia's 'refugee history' since the Second World War, belong to this history. Gadi Benezer and Roger Zetter admit surprise that the significance of the journey of migration as a life-changing and momentous event has had such scarce attention by scholars. 'The study of refugees focuses on either one end or the other of the migration process,' they write. 'What happens in between – the actual exilic process, the medium that connects the two ends – is largely forgotten or ignored.'[15] As we found when embarking on this project, many journeys lasted years, with false starts, detours and returns, prompting us to rethink the global map of Australian migration as one that has as many back doors and multiple entry points, as it does conventional routes and pathways.

We also found that the methods facilitating illegal movement varied depending on the circumstances of what was required. People smuggling is an industry of documents as much as it is of boats, planes and trucks. To cross borders illegally, people needed more than vehicles willing to take them, or officials willing to be bribed. Alien smuggling also involved the manufacture of fake passports, identity documents and travel visas. It involved deliberate defiance of ethnic migration sponsorship rules and racist quota restrictions on the part of brave or corrupt officials, by leaving names off lists, or on lists, or simply turning a blind eye. In every sense, people smuggling has functioned as a business modelled precisely on the legal system it sought to subvert.

Les Murray's story, recounted in Chapter 3, inspired the idea for this volume, but the knowledge that were it not for people smugglers neither of us would be here drove us to write it. In the first two chapters of this book, we each recount new histories of people smuggling dating back to the Holocaust and its aftermath, the period during which our own families came to Australia. Jews who escaped the Holocaust were often helped across borders, from France into Switzerland, or Spain, or from Austria or Germany, into China. After the Second World War, non-Jews fled Communist Eastern Europe by foot, truck or train, into displaced persons camps in Germany and Austria, where Australian agents facilitated their migration. Meanwhile, Jewish survivors who were excluded from

Australian refugee resettlement schemes because of anti-Semitism, used Australian Jewish contacts to illicitly procure landing permits.

The rest of the stories told in this book roughly follow a chronology of war and displacement from the Cold War through to the present. During the Hungarian uprising of 1956 and the Prague Spring, East Europeans sought a way to escape to the West, and were helped by those who knew where to find the cracks in the Iron Curtain. In the 1970s, Australians were introduced to the term 'boat people', as Vietnamese fled civil war, some of them in small boats across the seas that separated Southeast Asia from the northern Australian coastline. And to this lineage can be added, most recently, people from countries in Africa and the Middle East running from famine and violence.

These chapters each centre around the journey of one person or family. In Chapter 5 Nathalie Nguyen draws on oral histories she conducted with a number of women who had escaped Vietnam by boat after the Vietnam War. In Chapter 7 artist Phuong Ngo offers a rich photographic essay to trace his father's incredible journey from Vietnam to Australia, where he acted first as a smuggler himself in order to raise the money he needed to then pay another smuggler to take him and his family to safety. Chapter 13 is a collaborative effort between Claudia Tazreiter, Behrouz Boochani, an Iranian writer and activist who was detained in Papua New Guinea after coming to Australia by boat, and Boochani's translator, Omid Tofighian. The rest of the chapters are written by our authors, in close collaboration with us, or recounted to us, over a series of conversations. None had ever been asked the question of whether they remembered who their smuggler was, or their memories of the time 'in-between' leaving and coming to Australia. These personal accounts tell of experiences that are breathtaking in their bravery, their compassion, their perseverance and their survival. Taken together, they combine to tell a twentieth-century history of war and displacement rarely heard in the annals of

Australian migration history, but which also offer new insights into the liminal world of mountain passes, oceans, airports and islands that make up this illegalised geography of the asylum seeker and the refugee.

1

ESCAPING THE HOLOCAUST BY BREAKING THE LAW: COURAGE AND DISOBEDIENCE

Julie Kalman

The Second World War began on 3 September 1939. On 1 September, Germany had invaded Poland. Britain and France, who had given Poland a guarantee of protection of their border, declared war on Germany two days later. But they did not stop the German advance: the Polish army was defeated in a matter of weeks, and Warsaw, the capital, surrendered on 27 September. At the same time, the Soviet Union launched an invasion from the east. Poland was occupied, and partitioned, shared out according to the terms secretly agreed, as part of the German–Soviet Pact of 1939.

In 1940, Hitler turned his attention to Western Europe. In April, German forces conquered Denmark and Norway. Over May and June, in a campaign that lasted less than six weeks, German forces invaded and conquered the Netherlands, Belgium, Luxembourg and France. Paris fell on 14 June 1940. By mid-1940, German troops occupied much of Europe, and much of Europe's Jewish population was trapped. Nazi occupiers and local collaborators began the process of isolating Jews from society, building ghettos in the east, and putting anti-Jewish laws in place in the West. Safe havens for Jews in continental Europe were few. The journey to them was dangerous and difficult. Non-Jews who sought to help Jews, either to hide or to run, risked their own lives, and those of their family. In this chapter, I tell the story of some of the lucky ones, the Jews who found someone willing to defy the law; to smuggle them across a border, or to give them documents which allowed them to then smuggle themselves. Some of these smugglers were also Jews. As Ruth Balint describes in the next chapter, anti-Jewish immigration policies were in place in Australia after the war. Nonetheless, all of these lucky ones were able to settle here after the war, and to make new lives, bringing culture, and colour, to post-war Australia. In the 1990s, they recorded their testimonies with the University of Southern California Shoah Foundation Archive, founded by the film director Steven Spielberg. I draw from that archive in this chapter, to tell their stories.

Masha

When the Germans invaded Poland, many Jews fled to the relative safety of the Soviet-occupied area. Masha Frydman was born in Sosnowiec, in western Poland, in 1927. Her family knew that the Germans meant danger. She recalled: 'My father kept on constantly – as long as I can remember – he kept on saying that if the Germans will come here, we will have to run away.'[1] After the invasion, they found themselves in the German-occupied zone. They began to plan their flight across the Bug River, which formed the western border of the Soviet-occupied area. But they had heard rumours: 'thousands of people died swimming the river and thousands of people returned back and were shot by the Germans'.[2] Her father found a smuggler. Winter had come, and the river was frozen. The smuggler promised to take them across, a journey of seven kilometres. With her parents and two younger siblings, they made the crossing, and reached the Russian side on 1 January 1940. 'From far away, we heard singing. We heard Russian songs. And we thought that it's the Russian part. And after walking another few kilometres, we came to a little village. And then we were told that this is the Russian part, which was wonderful for us. So it meant life.'[3] It was to mean life for the Frydmans, but not at all as they had imagined. Soon after the Soviet Union annexed eastern Poland, the regime began a program of mass deportations. Polish Jews, as well as ethnic Poles, were taken from their homes with little notice, and put on cattle cars, which transported them to Siberia, deep inside the Soviet Union. As refugees from western Poland, Masha, her two siblings and her parents were counted among the civilians deemed undesirable.

They spent 18 months in a prison camp, surviving the winter by stealing potatoes from peasants. Masha and her brother would dig them out of the frozen ground, underneath a layer of snow. In 1941, after Germany invaded the Soviet Union, the family was allowed to leave. They chose to travel due south, seeking a warmer climate that would mean easier survival. They came to Kazakhstan and spent the war there. In 1949, Masha, now married to Abram Zeleznikow, received a permit to travel to Australia with her husband and father. In Melbourne, Masha and Abram bought a milk bar in Acland Street, St Kilda. Eventually this milk bar would become Scheherazade, a café that brought Eastern Europe, and its food and culture, to Australia. 'Australia was a terrible quiet place where everybody would stay at home.' With Scheherazade, Masha and Abram 'brought a lot of life to Acland Street.'[4]

Leopold

Leopold Zylberman, a Warsaw Jew born in 1915, also crossed the Bug River. Zylberman described what he called a 'smuggling industry' in the chaos of newly occupied Poland. People were bringing watches from the General Government across to the Germans, who were keen to buy them. From goods, it was just one step to the smuggling of people. The industry of smuggling people eastwards, and goods, both eastwards and westwards, was, in Leopold's words, 'blooming'. 'There were hundreds of smugglers.' Leopold himself, together with his new wife, Lola, his brother, sister-in-law, and a couple of friends, were taken in a goods truck, hidden under hay and merchandise. This was their first experience, but they went from smuggler to smuggler as their journey advanced, across the Bug River that separated the German from the Russian zone, and north to Bialystok. From there, more smugglers helped them to cross the border into Lithuania. It was Christmas. They were in a group of eight people, walking at night, through the snow. They had to take care to walk exactly in one another's footsteps. If someone were to pass through the snow after them, seeing just one set of footprints, they would not imagine that a group had been smuggled. On New Year's Eve, as Masha was crossing the Bug River with her family, they came to the border. The guards were busy celebrating in the station, so the group crossed. They ran, through the snow, and they did not stop until they came to a village. There, they rested in the cemetery. For Leopold, the smugglers were a 'terrific organisation', people 'who just made a living'.[5]

Many Polish Jews were able to make their way to Lithuania, still an independent state. This influx swelled the numbers of Jews in Lithuania to 250 000, or ten per cent of the population. In June 1941, Germany launched Operation Barbarossa, the German invasion of the Soviet Union. For Jews in Lithuania, there was nowhere to run. German forces advanced rapidly. More than three and a half million troops were supported by 3400 tanks and 2700 aircraft. It was the largest invasion force ever seen. In three weeks, the tanks covered 804 kilometres. Russia was literally invaded overnight. Jews in eastern Poland, the Baltic States of Lithuania and Latvia and the western Soviet Union could no longer escape.[6]

Over the course of three years, after they occupied it in 1941, German forces, helped by Lithuanian auxiliaries, murdered 90 per cent of the Jews in Lithuania. But in June 1940, in the days before the Soviet invasion of the country, desperate Polish refugees in Kaunas, the temporary capital, made their way from one foreign consulate to the next, seeking a precious visa which would mean escape. Leopold, like thousands of others, had the extraordinarily good fortune to come within the aegis of the Japanese consul, Chiune Sugihara. Late in 1939, Sugihara, a career diplomat who spoke fluent Russian, had opened the first Japanese consulate in Kaunas. His brief was to monitor German–Soviet relations. Sugihara quickly realised that the Jews in Lithuania, both refugees from Poland and Lithuanian Jewry, faced a desperate, dangerous situation. Starting in August 1940, Sugihara issued transit visas to all comers, whether or not they had documents, be that a landing visa, or even a passport. He was seconded by the honorary Dutch consul, Jan Zwartendijk, who would add a landing visa for Curaçao, a Dutch–Caribbean island. Sugihara's visas, valid for ten days, allowed Jews to transit through Japan to safe destinations. They also meant, therefore, that holders of the Japanese transit visa had the right to leave the Soviet Union. Refugees had to find – and often bribe – their way onto a train travelling across the Soviet Union to Vladivostok, a journey of about ten days. From there, they would take a boat to Kobe in Japan, the path followed by Leopold, with his wife, Lola. In Kobe, the Polish ambassador organised help for Sugihara's Jews, acquiring visas for them to travel onwards to final, safe destinations.

As dozens, and then hundreds of Polish Jews began to arrive in Japan, equipped with visas issued by Sugihara, the foreign ministry in Tokyo began to send urgent telegrams, ordering him to stop.[7] But Sugihara continued, now in direct violation of the instructions of his superiors. Through August 1940, Sugihara produced a month's worth of visas each day. In late August, with Lithuania now under Soviet control, Sugihara was ordered to close the consulate and move to his next posting in Berlin. But as he made his way from his hotel to the station, he continued to write visas, and as his train was pulling out of Kaunas station, he threw blank sheets of paper with the consular seal and his signature, which could be written up as a visa, into the crowd.

It is thought that he issued some six thousand visas to Jews, many of whom, as heads of households, were able to take their family on the visa. As many as ten thousand people would have been the fortunate recipients of his visas, although not all left Lithuania in time. Hillel Levine, who researched Sugihara's life, believes that no more than half of those were able to profit from Sugihara's rule breaking, and leave.[8]

In Kobe, Leopold set about obtaining a landing visa for a final destination for him and Lola. At the Polish Embassy in Kobe, those with money to pay for transport, could buy a visa to a desirable destination. Leopold was hoping for Canada or Australia, but he was low on the list for preferential treatment. Leopold's older brother was able to obtain a visa for Burma, promising to arrange for Leopold and Lola to join him and his wife there. But the Japanese, tired of waiting, arranged transport for the remaining Jews to Shanghai. It was possible to enter Shanghai without a landing permit, or entry papers, and more than twenty thousand Jews, refugees from Nazi Europe, spent the war years there. Many of those had received the transit visas that enabled them to travel to Shanghai from Sugihara. Others were given a similar visa by Ho Feng-Shan, the Chinese consul general in Vienna. He, too, disobeyed direct orders to issue more than four thousand visas. Leopold and Lola arrived there in late August or early September 1941.

In Shanghai, Leopold found work as a bookkeeper. He and Lola survived the Japanese invasion and subsequent incarceration in the Shanghai ghetto, tuberculosis (Leopold), and the American bombing of the city. In 1946, they departed for Australia, with a permit obtained through friends of his brother who were already there. In Melbourne, Leopold established first one clothing business, and then another. He and Lola had a daughter.

Stephen

Even when smugglers took money, they also took risks. As a young boy, Stephen Muller was smuggled away from certain death in a ghetto in Poland to the relative safety of a Hungarian village. Stephen's father owned a hardware store in Bochnia, in southern Poland, and it was through non-Jewish friends that he was able to organise the family's escape, first hidden in a mail van, and then on foot, across the Tatra Mountains, the mountain range that forms the border between Poland and Slovakia. These smugglers also took money, but, as Stephen pointed out, 'it was easier to take the money and become an informant of the Gestapo than to take the money and try and let you escape. And if you – and if you were taken, you know, you were also shot, but with the Jew.' The family spent two weeks crossing the mountain range, walking at night, and sleeping in huts during the day. One night, as the family crossed the mountains, Stephen became separated from his parents. 'I couldn't scream,' he remembered, 'I was not allowed to speak or scream or say anything. I was just supposed to walk.' Stephen, five years old, alone and lost in pitch dark, sat down and waited. And the guide, a Polish woodsman, came back and picked him up. 'I was never so happy to see anybody, I think. But he came back for me. He could have left me behind, I suppose.'[9]

Stephen and his parents travelled to Hungary, where they hid in a village outside Budapest until they were liberated by Russian forces, who arrived very shortly after German soldiers had come to the village and discovered the Muller family. Stephen was eight years old, and having survived, he was to spend more than three years moving from Bucharest, to Paris, to Connecticut, before finally settling in Sydney. Stephen studied medicine and became a surgeon.

Paul

On the other side of Europe, in Scheveningen, in the Netherlands, Paul Kornmehl and his family followed the progress of the German army very closely. The Kornmehls were Jews from Eastern Europe who had moved to Holland in 1916. Paul was the youngest of four children, with a brother and two sisters, both married. His parents were religiously observant Jews. The Kornmehls, like many other Dutch Jews, did not believe that Germany would attack Holland, so when the attack did come, in May 1940, they were shocked, and frightened. Holland was occupied in a matter of days, and then Belgium, and the north of France. To the north, Denmark and Norway were occupied, too. Western Europe was blocked. Only Switzerland and Spain seemed safe, protected by the mountain ranges that formed their borders.

Escape to the safety of Switzerland, or Spain, or even Eastern Poland, was impossible without the help of middlemen. These were locals, who knew the back ways across the mountain ranges that isolated Spain and Switzerland, or the safe way across the Bug River, and who were prepared to smuggle refugees across those borders for a payment. Or they were a tiny handful of foreign diplomats still in occupied Europe, so few in number that every Holocaust historian can name them, who broke rules and defied explicit instructions, issuing visas to Jews that allowed them to smuggle themselves across borders into safety. Under German occupation the law was mad, and it was murderous, but it was law nonetheless. To break this law and to risk death was the only way to escape almost certain death.

Before his departure, in the Netherlands, Paul and his family had listened to the radio, and heard about the treatment of Jews in Germany. He and his family remained convinced that they would be safe in Holland. But Germany did attack Holland, on 10 May 1940. 'We were occupied by the Germans in no time. We saw them marching within a few days.' Paul's and his father's business was Aryanised: taken over by a German. It was he who made it clear to Paul that he should flee. Paul took him at his word. 'Don't forget, 1940, they occupied nearly the whole of Europe. And before Holland, it was Norway. It was Denmark before Holland. And we were looking for a way out. To go to England was nearly impossible. So the only way of getting away was going from Holland to Belgium. And from Belgium to occupied France. From occupied France to unoccupied France, and either to Switzerland or to Spain.' On 24 November, Paul packed some food, and left with his girlfriend Melita, and another two couples. The three couples hired bicycles, and rode for three hours, until they came close to the Belgian border. A farmer showed them the place to cross on his land. From there, they went to Antwerp, then on to Brussels, where they spent three nights in a brothel. Anyone going to a hotel was required to show papers, and to register. But in the brothel, Paul and Melita slept in safety, protected by the madam, while German officers were getting to know the local population in the neighbouring rooms. From Brussels, they travelled by train to Liesle, a small town in eastern France, near Dijon. Here, they were to rendezvous with a smuggler who would lead them on a six-hour walk, over the line that demarcated occupied from Vichy France.

But Paul and Melita faced new troubles: Vichy France was 'worse than occupied France'. Paul's sister Anna, already in Marseille, organised *sauf-conduits* for the pair – the passes that allowed them to travel legally within France. They made their way to Lyons, and it was here that Paul enjoyed a stroke of good fortune. In Lyons, he found Maurice Jacquet, a Frenchman acting as the honorary Dutch consul in that city. For Paul, who had travelled, in constant danger, from the Netherlands, Jacquet was 'the most wonderful man I've ever met in my life'. Jacquet issued documents to desperate Dutch refugees – some Jewish, others not – which allowed them to travel safely within France, and get to border areas. Through Jacquet, Paul met others, including a man who was able to obtain the precious stamp that allowed Paul and Melita to stay legally in Lyons. The same stamp was used, as a sort of landing visa, to smuggle the rest of the family out of Holland: his other sister and her family, his brother and his wife, and his parents.

Paul spoke fluent French, and he was resourceful. He became a smuggler. In Lyons, he was able to buy a legal visa. In his sister's hotel in Marseilles, the Hotel Select, he set up a printing machine in the toilet, 'And we made visas for Mexico. We made visas for Panama. We made visas for all countries, not for money for us and for friends. And at the end, we made a visa, the *sortie*, which means an exit permit.' The family prepared to leave. His sister Anna, with her husband and daughter, travelled first to Perpignan, on the Mediterranean coast, near the French–Spanish border. There, they paid $1000 to hire an ambulance, which transported them to the Pyrenees, where the smuggler awaited them. But, Paul says, they made a mistake: they paid him half immediately. Here was a smuggler who was happy to take advantage of his clients. He took them up into the mountains. Once they reached a high point, he took the other half of the payment and disappeared. The family had agreed to contact Paul, still in France, once they reached Barcelona, but no news came. In early October, Paul and Melita, armed with their home-made counterfeit transit visas, made their way to the Pyrenees. In Pau, west of Perpignan, at the foot of the mountain range, Paul presented his Spanish visa to the consul. 'And the man said, my God, that is a very, very good forgery. And I said to him, my mother, my father, my brother, my brother-in-law, a child, cousin – they're all waiting for me, and I haven't heard from them. It all depends if you give me that stamp. The man looked into my eyes, and he gave me the stamp.' Paul and Melita crossed into Spain on their officially endorsed illegal visas, and made their way to Barcelona. There, they were reunited with Paul's family. It was early 1943.

After the war, Paul and Melita re-established themselves in Holland. With a friend, he went back into the hosiery business, using a factory in Czechoslovakia. Circumstances were to make a smuggler of Paul once again. In early 1948, Communists took over Czechoslovakia. Paul wished to help members of the Jewish community there, who wanted to leave. He used the trucking company that transported his pantyhose, Van Gend and Loos, hiding Jews inside the trucks. But the growing Cold War meant that business agreements with Czechoslovakia became increasingly difficult, and finally, impossible. It was the Cold War, and fear of what might ensue, that decided Paul and his family – and many other Jewish survivors – to leave Europe, once and for all. They arrived in Sydney in November 1952. Paul did what he knew best: he started a hosiery company that was to become enormously successful. It was called Kolotex.

Georges Mora and Marcel Manger

Jews were smuggled to safety, by opportunistic locals along the river Bug, and by Polish woodsmen. They were helped to smuggle themselves across continents and borders by sympathetic consuls, who had the power to issue visas, or to give them an all-important stamp, small pieces of paper that saved thousands of lives. Others, like Paul, acted as the smugglers. Georges Mora and his wife, Mirka, arrived in Melbourne in 1951. They, like Paul and Melita, were Jewish survivors who feared the prospect of a nuclear war. They had survived in France. They brought vibrancy and cosmopolitanism, and no small amount of cheekiness, to beige post-war Melbourne. They quickly became involved with Melbourne's art community, and established themselves in hospitality. First, Mora opened Café Balzac, a bistro in East Melbourne, which 'introduced Melbournians to authentic French provincial cooking'.[10] Then, in 1965, the couple bought the Tolarno Hotel in Fitzroy Street, St Kilda. The building housed them and their sons, as well as a restaurant, a private hotel, and a gallery. Mirka Mora decorated the restaurant walls. Tolarno Gallery became an intrinsic part of Melbourne's art scene. Georges died in 1992. Mirka died in 2018, aged 90.

In the Second World War, Georges Mora was someone else entirely. Mora was born Günter Morawski in Leipzig, in 1913. When Hitler came to power, Morawski, being Jewish, was no longer able to continue his studies in medicine at Berlin University. He went to Paris, and when the Germans invaded France in June 1940, Mora fled to the unoccupied zone, and joined the French Resistance. He organised a fake ID, and changed his name to Georges Morand, altogether much more French-sounding. But the Jewish orphans he cared for called him Mora, the name he kept after the war. In the Resistance, Mora met a young Jewish man from Alsace, Marcel Mangel. Mangel was born in 1923, the child of Jewish immigrants from Poland. When the war broke out, he and his older brother Alain fled Strasbourg and joined the French Resistance. Alain organised a fake ID card for Marcel, with a name that would sound less Jewish. Marcel chose the name of a general from the French Revolution: Marceau.

After the war, Marcel Marceau would become world famous for his mime. During the war he used his artistic skills to save around a hundred Jewish orphans, by smuggling them across the border from Annemasse in France, to safety in Switzerland. Starting in early 1943, Marceau and Mora undertook nine convoys of children. The two men disguised themselves as nuns, and dressed the children in scout uniform, ready for a 'hike' in the Alps. Each child had lunch – a sandwich made on a baguette. Georges had observed that the German guards at the border did not open baguettes that had mayonnaise oozing out the side, for fear of getting grease on their gloves.[11] Mora sent out a memo to the Resistance, that all documents should be wrapped in wax paper and smothered in mayonnaise. This was the origin of his nickname, given him by the Resistance: 'Monsieur

Mayonnaise.' In 2016, George's son Philippe made a documentary, in which he followed in his father's tracks. In one scene, he meets Henri Parens, an eminent child psychiatrist living in Philadelphia. In 1943, as a young Jewish boy living in France, Parens was cared for and ultimately saved by Mora. Many of the children whose lives were saved by being smuggled across the Franco–Swiss border to safety found their way to the United States. The smuggler himself came with his wife to Melbourne in 1951, seeking a safe place to raise their own children, far from the Cold War.

Lola

Jews all over Europe smuggled, to save themselves or their loved ones, and this smuggling took many forms. Very often, these were small acts, illegal and defiant, decided on the spur of the moment as a way to buy life for a little longer, or to live better, for as long as life was allowed. Lola Snow was born Lola Majerczyk in 1922, in Bedzin, Poland. She was the only daughter, the second child of an older couple. Her father owned a bank, and the family was well to do. She was one of the many who made their way to Russian-occupied Poland after the war broke out. Lola fled with a boyfriend, leaving her mother in the German-occupied area. She ended up in Lvov, with her aunt and uncle. (The city is in Galicia, then southeastern Poland. At that time, the city was called Lvov; the Nazi occupiers renamed it Lemberg. Today it is called Lviv and located in Ukraine.) In Lvov, under Soviet rule, Lola worked and did well. She was even able to send money to her mother. Until, of course, mid-1941, when Lola became one of the many who were trapped by Operation Barbarossa. She ended up in the ghetto in Lvov. Lola had work cleaning German uniforms in a laundry, and she was able to leave the ghetto each day. In that way she made some money, which made life in the ghetto easier for her, her aunt and uncle, and her cousin, all there together.

And one day, when I came home from this laundry, there was a man there. And he – he handed me a little note. And on the note was written, please trust this man. And I recognise [sic] my mother's handwriting. And my mother sent him. She paid him most probably lots of money, because he was a smuggler – to smuggle me back to her, because between me and my mother was a border. Where I was, it was called the German protectorate. Where my mother was called the *Drittes Reich* [Third Reich]. And she thought, hearing what atrocities were going on in this part of occupied Poland, by the Germans, that I have more chance if I be with her. So she sent this man. And I trust him. I left my aunt. And I went with him. Don't ask me how long it took, how dangerous it was, and how many times we were nearly caught. But I reached my mother in December 1941 ... I returned back to Bedzin, to my mother. And I met my mother in the street. It was – it was a fantastic reunion.[12]

So, rather than join the many fleeing east, hoping to reach territories where there were no German occupiers, Lola moved back west, towards the enemy, in order to be with her mother, who had paid a fortune to a smuggler, to bring her daughter back. Lola crossed the border illegally, returning to danger to be with her mother. In Bedzin, living on the edges of the city, Lola had to hide, as she had no papers. But one day she was caught and taken to Oberaltstadt. This was a women's work camp, part of a network of camps around the town of Gross-Rosen, today Rogoźnica in Poland. There, she became a slave labourer in a cotton mill. This is where Lola spent the next three years and three months, surviving the transformation of the labour camp into a concentration camp. Her uncle, aunt, and cousin, who had stayed in the Lvov ghetto, were murdered along with most of the ghetto inhabitants. Lola married, and through her husband, whose sister was in Australia, they obtained a permit, and arrived in Sydney in November 1946.

Shaindl

Mothers took extraordinary risks to protect their children. In Poland, a stubborn woman named Shaindl refused to be separated from her children. She and her two sons were in a ghetto, in a town called Piotrkow. There were approximately 25 000 Jews there. In October 1942, German soldiers rounded up all of the Jews in the ghetto, an action, in the universe of evil euphemisms that National Socialism inhabited, called liquidation. They sent most of these Jews to Treblinka, a death camp, where most were murdered on arrival. But around two thousand Jews, who possessed work permits, were allowed to live. Shaindl had a place in this camp, and she smuggled her two sons, then aged six and eleven, in with her. A determined woman, she was good at finding the option at each turn that allowed you to live, even if just for a little longer. Shaindl kept her sons hidden, and even though the Nazis raided the smaller ghetto regularly, and shot anyone who was deemed to have no right to be there, the boys were never found. On one occasion, she put her younger son in the newly emptied receptacle that served as a toilet, pulled down her pants, and sat down there, refusing to budge when German soldiers raided. These were small acts of defiance and disobedience, acts that took extraordinary courage, because the price, had she been caught, would have been her death, and the death of her sons. Shaindl was liberated in Ravensbrück concentration camp, a women's camp near Bergen Belsen, in northern Germany. She had smuggled her younger son in with her, hidden in a sack that she carried. Her older son Arie, now aged 14, was taken to Buchenwald concentration camp, and put in the boys' block. Buchenwald was liberated by American soldiers on 11 April 1945, and Ravensbrück on 30 April, by Soviet soldiers advancing from the east. Shaindl found Arie's name on a Red Cross list of survivors.

Jews who were able to escape Nazi-controlled Europe make up the overwhelming majority of those who survived. Nowhere do statistics make this clearer than in Poland.[13] Before the war, the Jewish population in Poland was 3.3 million. This was the largest Jewish population anywhere in Europe, and the largest proportion of the broader population: Jews made up ten per cent of the number of people in the country. Historians estimate that about 350 000 Polish Jews of the original 3.3 million survived the Holocaust. Most of those survived by escaping across Russia, like Masha and Leopold. Shaindl, Arie, and her younger son, Peretz, were part of the four per cent of Polish Jews who spent much of the war in Poland, and who survived. In 1949, they came to Australia, and settled in Melbourne. They thrived: they studied, worked, married and raised children.

In her book *Reading the Holocaust*, Inga Clendinnen concludes with the poem 'Could Have' by the Polish Nobel Prize-winning poet Wislawa Szymborska. It is a poem, Clendinnen writes, that expresses much of what she had tried to say in the previous 200 pages:

It could have happened.
It had to happen. It happened earlier. Later.
Nearer. Farther off. It happened, but not to you.

You were saved because you were the first.
You were saved because you were the last.
Alone. With others.
On the right. The left.
Because it was raining. Because of the shade.
Because the day was sunny.

You were in luck – there was a forest.
You were in luck – there were no trees.
You were in luck – a rake, a hook, a beam, a brake,
A jamb, a turn, a quarter-inch, an instant ...[14]

Survival was largely a matter of chance. But survival also came from acts of disobedience, small or great, which in those extreme circumstances became acts of extraordinary courage and significance. The smuggling of Jews to safety – across borders, through Russia to Japan, into safe places – were such acts. It is because of one such small act that I am here. Shaindl, who survived in Poland and Germany through extraordinary luck, but also through stubbornness and defiance, was my grandmother, her son Arie, my father.

2

A JEWISH REFUGEE RACKET

Ruth Balint

In early 1950, Australian and British intelligence uncovered what they believed to be a Jewish racket in illegal immigration to Australia, operating out of Vienna and Sydney. Secret intercepts of correspondence between Australia and Austria suggested a sophisticated underground network of Jewish 'people smugglers' assisting Holocaust survivors to get to Australia. This was further backed up by Australian migration officials working in Munich, who wrote to Canberra warning that 'unsuitable and doubtful persons' were obtaining back-door permits with the assistance of Jewish welfare organisations in Australia. A secret memo from Australia's Chief Migration Officer based in Cologne, Noël Deschamps, to the Immigration Department Secretary in Canberra, THE (Ted) Hayes, also warned of a Jewish conspiracy to deceive Australian immigration officials, advising him that 'the average Jewish Landing Permit Holder can only be viewed with the gravest misgiving'.[1]

These fears were shared across the political establishment, and headlines appearing in Australian newspapers around this time had already whipped up considerable public anxiety about the existence of Jewish fraudsters gaming Australia's borders. In 1946, for example, NSW parliamentarian Jack Lang had thundered against the 'refugee racket' of 'wealthy' Germans and Austrians, a thinly veiled reference to Jews.[2] In 1949, explosive reports again surfaced in the Australian press detailing the existence of a Jewish smuggling ring circulating illegal landing permits. 'A group of black-marketeers is planning to fly 1000 illegal Jewish migrants to Australia', headlined the *Daily Telegraph* on its front page on 20 January 1949. 'French police say that a black-market ring has bought these landing permits from Jews, who received them from the Australian Government but were unable to use them. The ring has resold the permits to wealthier Jews', the article continued, noting that French police described the racket 'as one of the most daring black-market operations in Europe since the war'.[3] In October of the same year, newspapers again carried reports of a migrant racket that planned to bring 'hundreds of Central Europeans on faked immigration permit applications'. The story ran across several papers and several days, alleging that people in Australia, some of them in high positions, were signing landing permits for overseas applicants for a payment, and forging the signatures of officials and justices of the peace. The organisers were migrants themselves, 'a husband and wife who had been here 10 years, a Central European who arrived here less than two years ago', and a mystery third person.[4]

The fact that many Jewish survivors who wanted to come to Australia after the Second World War had to do so illegally was because Australian immigration policies were decidedly anti-Jewish in this period. This was mirrored in immigration policies across the English-speaking world. Fears of a Jewish influx of refugees were fuelled by pre-war xenophobia which had not diminished, despite the new knowledge of the horrors of the Holocaust. As discussed in the previous chapter, Jews were trapped in Europe partly because of the immigration policies of Western countries during the war, and these policies remained in practice if not in writing. 'We are not compelled to accept the unwanted of the world at the dictate of the United Nations or anyone else,' Liberal Member for Henty, Henry (Jo) Gullett told the Australian Parliament in 1946. 'Neither should Australia be the dumping ground for people whom Europe itself, in the course of 2,000 years, has not been able to absorb.'[5] These views did not represent everyone's but they were shared by enough of those in power to affect the ability of Jews to come to Australia in this period. More generally, the prejudice against Jewish migration was articulated as 'anti-reffo', often framed around the acute shortage in accommodation after the war that Jewish refugees were seen as potentially taking away from returned servicemen. Jewish leaders at the time noted the unjustness of these claims, but their attempts to right the record were drowned out by louder voices in parliament and the press.[6]

The first Immigration Department in Australia under the leadership of Arthur Calwell was established in 1945. Calwell's mandate was the creation of an immigration program to fill the country's desperate rural labour shortage, with an initial target of two per cent annual population increase. British migrants were the preferred type, but by 1946, it was clear that the British weren't coming in the numbers needed. Calwell turned to the Displaced Persons (DP) camps of Europe, where over a million refugees were looking to leave Europe for the West. By the end of the decade, over 170 000 European DPs had boarded ships to Australia, with free passage supplied by the International Refugee Organization (IRO). But in order to quell public anxieties about the possibilities of Jewish migrants coming in large numbers, Calwell imposed a quota by which Jewish refugees could not number more than 25 per cent on each refugee ship out of Europe. This was further lowered to 15 per cent in 1948, and was later extended to aeroplanes as well. In reality, however, it is unlikely that even these quotas were ever met. Australian migration officers tasked with screening eligible DPs were cautioned not to accept Jews and select only the kinds of people that Australians could 'consort with on Bondi Beach'. In the words of Migration Officer Harold Grant, Jews 'weren't replicas of the Bondi lifesaver as we wanted to make out about the "Beautiful Balts"'.[7]

Instead, the vast majority of Jewish refugees were forced to come to Australia as unassisted migrants with a landing permit. Getting a landing permit involved, firstly, being nominated, or sponsored, by someone in Australia using Form 40: more fully, 'Application for Admission of Relatives or Friends to Australia'.[8] As the title indicates, the sponsor had to be a friend or relative; in other words, known to the applicant. The sponsor also had to guarantee their nominee's work, accommodation and upkeep. Once this was approved, the landing permit was then forwarded to the individual or family waiting in Europe, who then had to undergo a medical screening (known as a Form 47) and secure berths on a ship to Australia. This process was supposed to ensure that only close family members would be admitted to Australia, but in 1950, Australian security and immigration officials began to raise the alarm in Canberra, with allegations about a black market in illegal landing permits. Stamped 'Top Secret', these intelligence reports detailed a smuggling racket operating between Vienna, Paris and Sydney in Australian landing permits for Austrian Jews.

Keith Turbayne was the main author of these top-secret reports. A young Australian military intelligence officer, Turbayne had arrived in Germany in 1949 with instructions to assist the head of the Australian Military Mission on security matters affecting the DP migration scheme. This was to mark the beginning of a long and close association between the Department of Immigration and the Army, and then, after 1951, the Australian Security and Intelligence Organisation (ASIO).[9] Turbayne and another army intelligence officer, Howard Miller, were sent to Cologne where the Australian Migration Office was based, under the supervision of Vincent Greenhalgh. They were given a small, cramped office in the attic, but much of their time was spent on the road, visiting and liaising with American and British intelligence in the Allied military occupation zones. Turbayne's area of responsibility was the US Zones in Germany and Austria, and he was determined to prove his intelligence credentials. His reports from Vienna were detailed, and included secret intercepts of letters and telegrams, as well as transcripts of phone taps, supplied by his friends in British and American military intelligence.

Writing to Greenhalgh in February 1950, Turbayne warned that 'there has been a great deal of manipulation and falsification of documents in regard to Landing Permit Holders'. The people involved were practically all Jews from Iron Curtain countries. 'They are generally interested in Black Market dealings and are known as Café inhabitants,' he wrote. 'They are not good types.'[10] They were also problematic from a security point of view. There were undoubtedly, in Turbayne's opinion, Communist sympathisers among the Jewish refugees. A few months after the first, Turbayne sent another report, in which he once again detailed the problem of illegal Jewish Landing Permit Holders, who were being assisted, he had learned, by Jewish welfare organisations in Europe and Australia. As long as a migrant had money to pay agents, he wrote, 'no difficulty was experienced in obtaining a permit'. This had 'provided a comparatively easy, if somewhat expensive means of access to Australia ... Many of these applicants particularly those from Hungary and to a lesser extent Czechoslovakia have admitted that they do not know nor have they ever heard of their sponsors in Australia. The sponsors are so often "a friend's friend".'[11]

The intercepts included in Turbayne's reports were certainly incriminating. Lily E in Paris wrote to Hilde W in Vienna with the address of an Australian, 'who can get a permit within 8 weeks for $300 and within 4 weeks for $360'. The address of the man, with a distinctly Jewish name, was in Mosman, Sydney. 'In the past, Australian visas were granted within a day,' she explained. 'Now it takes 4–6 weeks, because new enquiries are being made in Australia whether the passport has been falsified,' adding that 'The English are very finnicky when they find out such matters.' Lanci S of Cammeray warned his friend Ladislaus that the age limit for migrants was 42. 'You should be careful therefore with whom you are negotiating.

It is quite likely that you will have to make yourself younger than you really are.' Name changes were also advised so as to appear less Jewish. 'A friend of mine has done it all in the way that he changed over to another name by leaving out only one letter, for example from Schmeidl to Schmidl,' advised a Sydney resident to a friend in Vienna. 'The only important things here are the Passport and the Permit, you need no documents and if necessary, you can always say they were lost.'

Clearly the trade was viewed as profitable by some. 'Many people have earned a nice lot of money with this here for it is not a question of one or two but of twenty to thirty and it is settled in a hundred percent of cases,' Ignaz K of France ('Language: Jewish') wrote to Salomon G in Vienna. 'At the same time I must tell you it is a bit more difficult to do here because there are so many on the job.' A brother told his sibling in Melbourne about two friends in Vienna who were begging for a permit: 'They will pay you a good compensation if you could do that,' he wrote. 'I could find more of these people, but I do not know if you want to go into this matter. I think the profit will be more than your present job ... perhaps we could manage something while I am still here.' The rate for one of these illegal landing permits varied, according to another man in Vienna, Dr Artur W. 'As you probably know, amateurs asked for £350–400 and there are several who have provided permits for four–five families, a short time ago even a sixty-two-year-old man travelled with the permit he got.' But Frank K in Sydney wrote to Paul W in Vienna that he apparently knew of one man that could do it all for £180, and within two weeks.

These communications revealed an illegal Jewish migration racket that drew Australia into a global orbit that stretched from Sydney and Melbourne to major cities in Europe and South America. 'It is known that a net of agents exists in Hungary, America, Austria, Australia and France,' Turbayne wrote. The major centre of operations, he explained, was the Rothschild Spital, a Jewish staging centre in

Vienna for refugees, that had been a Jewish hospital before the war. Post-war Austria was certainly unique in terms of Jewish refugees. Its geographical location meant that many different groups of Jewish survivors passed through Austria leaving or returning home to countries in Eastern Europe after the war. These included Hungarian and Romanian Jews returning from concentration camps, Polish and Lithuanian Jews who were smuggled across European borders towards Israel, Romanian Jews who were escaping severe famine and dire living conditions, and those from Hungary and Czechoslovakia fleeing Communist takeovers in their countries. Austrian Jews liberated from Theresienstadt and other concentration camps, as well as returnees who had fled in 1938 after its annexation by the Third Reich swelled these numbers. In all, over 195 000 Jews passed through Austria between 1945 and 1950, some staying only for a few days before moving on. At least 169 000 of these were officially accommodated at the Rothschild Spital, mainly under the leadership of Bronislaw Teicholz, named in Turbayne's report as being of greatest concern, 'involved in many undercover activities and allegedly a very wealthy man. It is believed he has expressed the intention of emigrating to Australia. From all accounts a most undesirable character.'[12] Elsewhere, he was named as being in close connection with the Russians, organising black-market activities, and using his influence to get other Jewish black marketeers released from jail.

It is true that Teicholz had experience of forging identity documents and procuring false travel papers. In 1941 he escaped Lvov just before his parents and siblings were deported and murdered, joining a partisan group called Skole-Lawdezne and eventually fleeing across the border at Munkacz into Hungary, where he made contact with the underground Jewish community. He became the leader of the Polish Rescue Committee in Budapest, where he attempted to warn a disbelieving Jewish leadership of the Nazi plans for Jewish extermination and of what was happening to Polish Jews. After the

Nazi Arrow Cross takeover of Budapest and Hungary in 1944, he organised an underground group by the codename of Glick, with at least 120 Jewish men and women involved at any one time, which organised food and clothing for illegal Jewish refugees, and forged identity papers, baptismal certificates and passports.[13] His forgery operations led him into contact with Raoul Wallenberg, the most respected Swedish diplomat in Hungary whose main mission was rescuing Jews by issuing them with official prospective passes.

Years later in an interview, Teicholz described his secret meeting with Wallenberg in a Budapest café in 1944, on the eve of the 'Final Solution' in Hungary. Wallenberg knew that Teicholz was counterfeiting Swedish passes, which were considered the most valuable documents in terms of ensuring escape, but was concerned that these fake passes might jeopardise his ability to issue genuine ones to Jews with provable Swedish connections and official Hungarian approval.

However, according to historians Frederick Wurbell and Thurston Clarke, Wallenberg secretly approved of Teicholz's operation. Unlike Wallenberg's passes, which favoured the wealthier, educated and better connected Jews over those too poor to have any real connections with Sweden, Wurbell and Clarke write that Teicholz 'redressed the basic injustice of the protective passes':

> Teicholz dressed his blond Jewish fighters in the green uniforms
> of the Arrow Cross, the Hungarian fascist party. These bogus
> storm troopers then burst into the Jewish soup kitchens and
> raced up and down the rough wooden tables thrusting passes
> into the hands of every diner. They gave the passes to anyone who
> wanted them, to Jews who had never done business with Sweden,
> to poor Jews who had never travelled outside Budapest, and to
> uneducated Jews who did not know where Stockholm was.[14]

The meeting between the two men was brief. Wallenberg confronted Teicholz about his counterfeit operation, which Teicholz did not deny, reassuring Wallenberg that he was not selling them but giving them away to anyone who wanted one. Wallenberg promised to cover for him, only asking that he not print so many. According to the story given by Wurbell and Clarke, Teicholz agreed, and as soon as he left the meeting, told his lieutenants to print 15 000 Swedish passes.[15] The Nazi leadership put a price of 500 marks on Teicholz's head, but he survived, first going to Romania as part of the Hungarian Red Cross, and then to Vienna.[16] He became a central figure of Jewish self-organisation in Vienna, based at the Rothschild Spital from the end of the war until 1952 when he emigrated to the United States. Later he went on to receive the Ot Haganah award in Israel in 1967 and the State Fighters Award in 1988. He was recognised for having assisted nearly 200 000 Jews get medical aid, vocational training and travel assistance during his time as president of Rothschild Spital. In 1988 a Holocaust memorial was dedicated at the Dohany Utcai Synagogue in Budapest, where Teicholz received an award for his work on behalf of Hungarian Jewry.

In 1945, Wallenberg disappeared, possibly thought to have been murdered by the Soviets after the war. My grandfather Sándor Grozinger worked alongside Wallenberg in the Jewish resistance in Budapest, and likely knew Teicholz, perhaps well, though this is something I will likely never know. What is certain is that the illegal activities of men like Teicholz and my grandfather during the war saved many lives, and, after it, provided a secure haven and safe passage to the West.

At the same time that the screening and exclusion of Jews intensified in Australian immigration policy, ex-Nazis and fascist sympathisers appeared to be entering the country with ease. The Commonwealth Investigation Service warned Calwell fairly soon after refugee ships began arriving that there were former members of the SS among the DPs. Several who had arrived had scars under their armpits, indicating they had removed their SS tattoo, common practice by ex-Nazis smuggling themselves through the DP camps to the West. Calwell angrily dismissed the report as a 'farrago of nonsense', concerned that such reports would jeopardise his immigration policies.[17] By the end of the 1940s, Australia seemed less troubled by war criminals or ex-Nazis than by Jews or Communists. A secret 'Iron Curtain Embargo' was devised in 1949 to restrict people coming from the Iron Curtain countries, but behind the scenes, migration officers also viewed it as a way to keep out Jews. 'In view of the alarming increase in the number of Jews entering the Commonwealth,' the policy brief outlined, 'the Minister directed earlier this year that applications for the admission of Jews was to be delayed as far as possible.' But more direct measures were needed to stem the flow, and by restricting people coming from Iron Curtain countries (such as Hungary, Czechoslovakia and Poland), 'whose nationals comprise the majority of Jewish migrants', the government could claim it was not anti-Semitic, but merely preventing people who were potential 'security risks' from entering Australia.[18]

It is uncertain how far this kind of 'bureaucratic subterfuge' in Australia was felt in Central Europe. Officers tasked with implementing these vague instructions were already well versed in obstructing Jewish applicants as far as possible, and Jewish people were no strangers to dealing with obstructive officials. Most were well acquainted with having to negotiate their way through bureaucratic hoops to survive, even before the Holocaust, including resorting to illegal methods. For many Eastern European Jews, 'buying and selling on the black market, assuming fake identities and obtaining forged papers were ... facts of life'.[19] Joseph Roth, the Austrian Jewish writer and journalist, observed the experience of the recently arrived Eastern European Jew in Vienna, forced to register with the police. First, he had to show his papers, which were not like Christian papers.

'Christian papers are in order. All Christians have sensible, European names. Jewish names are mad and Jewish.' Their surnames were confusing, their birth dates inaccurate. In many cases the papers had been burned. 'So how did our man get across the border? Without a passport? Or even a false one? That means his name isn't even his real name – even though he gave so many of them, so many, in fact that they can't all be right.' In the end the police will decide to send him packing and come back with proper papers and sensible names. These official requirements for conventionally legal Jewish identities inevitably produced illegal ones:

> So he's sent packing, and again, and again, and again. Till it dawns on the Jew that he has no option but to give false information for the correct impression. To stick to one name that might not be his but would be a plausible and believable name anyway. The police have given the Eastern Jew the idea of concealing a true but tangled set of circumstances behind bogus but tidy ones.[20]

Roth died on the eve of the Second World War, but his astute description of 'the futile battle with papers' that consumed Jewish lives equally applied after the end of the war. 'The struggle for papers, the struggle against papers', Roth wrote, 'is something the Eastern Jew gets free of only if he uses criminal methods to take on society.'

Two years after Turbayne's original 1950 reports, another migration officer, WK McCoy, submitted an equally detailed indictment of the Jewish Landing Permit racket operating out of Vienna, which, he noted, 'had reached somewhat alarming proportions'. He listed various factors contributing to the illegal migration of Jewish Landing Permit Holders. Of concern was the fact that there were inadequate security checks for those coming from Iron Curtain countries. People were paying for fake medical x-rays, to cover up the incidence of TB or 'gross cosmetic defects', a reference to the strict exclusion of people with disabilities including minor cosmetic ones, under Australian immigration policy. Individuals in Australia were making a lucrative business in signing landing permits for people who were neither relative nor friend, 'in violation of the spirit and probably the letter' of immigration policy. 'Probably', because by the end of the 1940s, the line between what was considered legal and what was considered illegal in the landing permit procedure was already quite blurred. After 1948, the Australian Jewish Welfare Society was permitted to provide sponsorship and maintenance to Jewish (AJWS) landing permit applicants, provided it could provide enough suitable accommodation and living expenses. This resulted in a huge upsurge in Jewish applicants coming in under the auspices of the AJWS (approximately 17 763 between 1945 and 1954), and a backlash among migration officials who worried about the 'traffic in accommodation guarantees'.[21]

Finally, McCoy wrote, 'it should be pointed out that perhaps a majority of the applicants from Austria are people of middle European Jewish origin and while repudiating all anti-Semitic sentiments it can be strongly claimed that these individuals are anything but what one would like to envisage as permanent Australian settlers'. Employing anti-Semitic tropes nonetheless, he continued:

> Because of their background, occupation as 'Middlemen'
> financial agents etc, perhaps honest occupations in themselves,
> they are unsuited as future settlers and would tend rather to
> increase the category of non-productive citizens of which
> Australia has more than enough.[22]

These statements betrayed an ongoing adherence to a racial hierarchy in immigration practice that had long sought to exclude Jews as undesirable citizens in a White Australia. Race-based assumptions about assimilability that had structured attitudes to migrants and foreigners in Australia since Federation in 1901 hadn't disappeared after the Holocaust. Nor, as noted earlier, were these sentiments unique to Australia, though it is perhaps easy to understand why Jewish survivors wished to leave Eastern Europe, even in the face of restrictions and quotas in the West. Many who went back to their villages and towns in Eastern Europe after the war, to search for relatives, retrieve belongings or simply to go home, faced virulent anti-Semitism including pogroms, as well as official persecution. It was not unusual for many of Europe's Jews to spend several years waiting for news of family members before making the decision to leave. In Vienna, too, Jews were unable to stay with ease. In 1953, Austrian officials rejected an appeal by the Jewish organisation Agudat Israel to ease the process of naturalisation for Jews in Austria, countering that Jewish refugees 'in many cases demonstrate a poor capacity to assimilate ... The policy of the Austrian government agencies with respect to this group of refugees, who can only be assimilated with great difficulty, is to force them to emigrate.'[23]

The Australian Jewish community more than doubled in size between 1933 and 1950, mainly through the migration of Holocaust survivors after 1945. According to the federal census records, of declared Jews by religion, numbers rose from 23 553 in 1933 to 32 019 in 1947 and 62 208 in 1971. But if the number of those who did not declare their religion is taken into account, it is likely the numbers are far higher, with estimates for 1950 at 45 500 and for 1952 at 53 750, showing that in the peak years of Jewish migration after the war, Australian Jewry grew by 52 per cent.[24] It is unknown how many might have come here during that time using less-than-kosher landing permits, but it is likely that there were some. Their histories have been buried under the more palatable contemporary narrative of official Australian support for post-war Jewish migration in the wake of the Holocaust. But we might argue that the success of the Jewish migration program in the creation of a strong and vibrant community in Australia was in some ways down to Jews themselves here and overseas, rather than the Australian Government. Like other survivors of war and conflict who sought out Australia as a safe haven, some of the Jewish refugees of post-war Europe, faced with the reality of racially based immigration restrictions in Australia and anti-Semitism in Europe, smuggled themselves here. 'Never again', which became a Jewish mantra after the war, may have had more meanings than one.

3

LES MURRAY:
WE WOULD HAVE HAD A BEER

Julie Kalman

Les Murray was known to many in Australia as Mr Football. For 35 years, he presented the round-ball game – or, as he preferred to call it, the world game – to viewers on SBS. Football was Les Murray's passion, and he devoted his life to sharing this passion with Australians, relative latecomers to the world of football. He hosted no less than eight Football World Cups. But there was more than just football to Les's story. Les came to Australia from Hungary with his parents and two brothers in 1956. How he got there is a story of extraordinary danger and generosity. Les Murray passed away in 2017, following a long illness. He was 71. This chapter draws on his autobiography and on a documentary he made for the SBS current affairs program Dateline *in 2011.*

Les Murray was born László Ürge in 1945, to a family that had belonged to the Hungarian elite. The Ürge family lived in Budakeszi, a small village near Budapest. Hungary was part of the Eastern Bloc in the Cold War, ruled by a repressive Communist regime, in thrall to Soviet Russia. But in 1956, when Les was nearly 11, unprecedented events in Hungary changed his life. On 23 October, peaceful student demonstrations in the capital, Budapest, escalated into an armed insurrection against the repressive regime and the occupying Soviet forces. Protesters tore down a statue of Stalin, removed Soviet red stars from buildings, and cut out the Soviet emblem from the middle of the tricolour Hungarian flag. Hungarian Communist sympathisers and members of the detested security forces were beaten and executed in the streets. From their two-bedroom flat in Budakeszi, the Ürge family followed events avidly.

A ceasefire was declared on 28 October, and the Soviet forces that had occupied Hungary since 1944 began to withdraw from Budapest. It seemed that the revolt had succeeded, and euphoric crowds celebrated. But on 4 November, the Kremlin launched Operation Whirlwind. Soviet tanks returned to the streets of Budapest, and the revolution was crushed mercilessly. Two thousand five hundred Hungarians were killed in the fighting, and in the aftermath, many thousands were arrested and tried. Reprisals against the revolutionaries took place with equal violence. As former members of the Hungarian elite, and supporters of the uprising, the Ürge family found themselves targeted. Boys of Les's age threw rocks at the family's balcony. Les's parents had lost all hope of ever seeing a democratic Hungary, and they decided that their only choice was to leave. The brutal crackdown triggered a mass exodus of Hungarians seeking refuge in the West. Large numbers of people fled the country, and the Ürge family were among them. In his autobiography By the Balls: Memoir of a Football Tragic, *Les told the story of his family's flight.*[1] *It was a cold winter morning in December, when Les was woken early by his mother.*

It was bitterly cold and uncomfortable

'Wake up. We're going,' she said. 'Going where?' I asked. It was 2 am. Much too early for school. 'Never mind. Just get dressed. Quick.' Obediently, we moved swiftly in the dead of night. We were hauled, all five of us, onto the back of a truck. It was bitterly cold and uncomfortable. But we sat in silence. The truck took us to one of Budapest's three major railway stations: the one that services the West, the route to the Austrian border.

Les's parents had made plans to flee together with their neighbours, the Keresztes family: a couple and two young children. Unbeknown to the young Les, his parents, together with the Keresztes family, had made contact with a broad network of conspirators, including people near the border, who were prepared to hide and help the two families for payment. On that fateful morning, the Ürge family set out on a two-day journey to the village of Pinkamindszent, a kilometre from the Austrian border. They hoped to get past checks and roadblocks with the story that they were travelling to attend a country wedding, visiting old friends along the way.

The penny dropped: we were defecting

Once we were on the train the penny dropped: we were defecting. We were about to become dissidents. Refugees. For years, I had been listening to my parents talking about getting out, escaping: finding a way to a new life of freedom and some kind of bliss. This was no desperate run for the border. It was a meticulously planned conspiracy, devised in collusion with our neighbours, the Keresztes family, a young couple with two small children, who took the same journey. The Keresztes couple and my parents were the only people who knew the plan: with the secret police hovering, they told no one. My parents, bless their souls, were a lot smarter than I knew at the time.[2]

It was a crime to defect. Defectors faced harsh punishments, including forced labour, imprisonment, torture and death. This was a journey fraught with danger, and the family was understandably anxious to ensure that their lie was not exposed. There was a strong police presence along the family's route. The authorities were aware, of course, that tens of thousands of Hungarian citizens were trying to flee. Their train moved on, towards the western border.

Too many Russians

Uniformed men would board at each stop, check IDs, and ask questions. The authorities were not stupid. At one point, the train passed through the station of Székesfehérvár, a major city between Budapest and the Austrian border. From a train heading in the other direction, people leaned out of their windows and screamed to us: 'Forget it. There are too many police. Too many Russians. You will be turned back!'[3]

But the family pushed on, and this was a choice that almost cost them dearly. The family's first stop was to be the city of Körmend, in Hungary's west. As their train drew near, it was stopped and the Hungarian secret police boarded. Les's family was taken off the train and transported to a nearby barracks. His father was taken away and interrogated for six hours, while Les, his two brothers, and his mother waited, locked in a bare room. Their relief, when he was eventually released, and they were permitted to leave, was great. The family spent one night in Körmend, and the next morning, they prepared for the final leg of their journey.

Our final leap

We were to be taken to a small village by horse and cart, disguised as a peasant family going to a peasant wedding. The Keresztes family would follow the next day ... Subdued, scared, crumpled humbly under blankets in the back of the cart, we set off for our last stop before negotiating our final leap to the promised land.[4]

Their final stop was the village of Pinkamindszent, just one kilometre from the Austrian border. Here, they encountered a roadblock. Two Russian soldiers manned a checkpoint, their job to detect and arrest would-be defectors. With their story of the country wedding, and dressed as farmers, the family got through. They made their way to their final contacts, the Orbàn family. Here, they met a tall, thin young man called Gyula, or Julius (in his autobiography, Les calls him Louis). He was the young son of the Orbàn family, and it would be his job to walk the Ürges to the border at midnight. They were ushered into the Orbàn home, where Julius's family awaited them. Here, the Ürges found that new demands were to be made on them.

They expect to be paid for their service

After small talk and coffee, the negotiations began. What could we pay for this service? What did my parents have, if anything, that might represent the right price? Years later, I realised that, however unkind our hosts might have seemed at the time, this was the way of things when one decides to be a refugee. One sets forth in the darkness on a precarious adventure over roads full of potholes, where dangers lurk at every corner, where lives of children are at stake, where no stranger can be trusted, where there is an essential need to rely on help from those who know the potholes and the dangers and who are experts at negotiating them. These people in more scornful, modern parlance, are known as people traffickers. But the expression, in my view, is unkind, given that it reflects far too disparagingly on people who are an essential part of the refugee process: people without whom successful quests for freedom would be impossible. They expect to be paid for their service, a fact that is neither unusual nor particularly relevant in the big scheme of things.

My parents began to peel off whatever they had: cash, jewellery, valuable clothing.[5]

But when the father of the family made to take Les's mother's thick winter coat as part of the payment, Julius intervened.

The family was to face a final great danger. The Keresztes family, who were to have followed them one day later, had come early. The Russian soldiers at the checkpoint believed the story of the wedding once, but not twice, and the Keresztes, and the driver of the cart, were arrested. The Russian soldiers might return to search for them, and the Ürges had to hide. Julius took them to the grange behind the house, and they spent four hours there, hidden under hay, until Julius came to fetch them. It was finally time to leave.

An agent of conspiracy

Out of the still night came the knock on the gate and the voice of Louis. We climbed down from under the hay, shook ourselves off and got ready, placing our future into Louis'[s] hands. The clock showed midnight as we set off for the border: our family of five, and Louis. It was a dangerous walk for all of us, but Louis took the greatest risk. If we were caught he would surely go to jail, as assisting defectors was a serious crime, much greater than attempting to defect. The night was still and cold, the terrain pancake flat. A cover of shallow snow illuminated the sky. Visibility was good, a mixed blessing, given that it made us more vulnerable to being spotted by the frontier guards, perched high in their lookout towers a few hundred metres apart.

Louis allowed my parents to lead and walked at the back of the group, holding the hands of the two youngest boys: Joe and me. Nobody spoke. The rhythmic crackling of snow under our feet was the only noise to interrupt the stillness. We saw the vague, intimidating outlines of the towers in the distance. But they were far away. Louis knew the terrain well, and the best and safest way to slip between the guards. We heard shots in the distance. Louis told us not to be alarmed, for they were only shooting in the air. The towers were manned by Hungarian soldiers who were, in the main, sympathetic to the cause; their sporadic shooting was aimed less at refugees than at impressing their commanders.

We walked for what seemed like an eternity but was probably no more than half an hour, until Louis commanded us to stop. He told us we had already crossed the Hungarian border and we were now in no man's land, a buffer of a few hundred metres between frontiers. Louis said this was as far as he could go. He gave us instructions to keep walking in the same direction, saying that after a kilometre or so we would encounter an Austrian village. He embraced and kissed each of us, said goodbye, turned around and headed back to Pinkamindszent, his figure, as we stood and stared, slowly disappearing into the night.

Louis was an agent of conspiracy, a 'people trafficker', helping the captive and the helpless negotiate a precarious avenue to freedom. He was, I believe, genuinely on our side and, to this day, remains a hero for me.[6]

The family walked on, until they heard voices in the distance.

They were singing

Finally, we got close enough to approach the source of the noise, for noise rather than music is mostly what it was. It was a pair of Austrian drunks, happily staggering home from a long night at the local *keller*...

My father told the two men who we were, what journey we were on and why we were trudging through the snow in the dead of night. One of the drunks broke into loud laughter, slapped my father on the back and slurred: 'Well, welcome. You are free.'[7]

The Ürge family spent five months in Austria, in an army barracks converted into a refugee camp near Salzburg. This was Camp Roeder, an American-built installation. It became known for receiving Hungarians, seen by the Western world as freedom fighters. The uprising, and its brutal suppression, garnered much sympathy among Western audiences. This was a story that fit snugly into a Cold War narrative, where hapless

Hungarians fought for their democratic freedom, against the Soviet juggernaut. The Hungarian freedom fighter was Time Magazine's *Man of the Year. News of the events in Hungary had spread rapidly around the world. The UNHCR was the main organisation involved in managing the needs of the Hungarian refugees arriving in Austria. They appealed to UN member states for assistance: Australia, among other Western countries, was quick to respond. Just three days after the call for help was made, the Australian Government offered permanent asylum to 3000 Hungarian refugees, and a contribution to the cost of travel. There was general support among the Australian public for the Hungarian refugees. This was the first intake of several, and ultimately, over 14 000 'Fifty-sixers' were offered settlement in Australia.*

The Ürge family were among them. In early May 1957, six months after they had left Hungary, the Ürge family were informed that they had been accepted into Australia. From Salzburg, they travelled by bus, north to Linz. From there they boarded a plane, a four-engine turbo prop, which required no less than five refuelling stops on its way to Darwin. From Darwin, the family was flown to Wagga Wagga, in New South Wales. The final leg of their journey took them 150 kilometres south to Bonegilla, near Wodonga.

Bonegilla had been established as a reception and training centre for migrants by the Australian Department of Immigration, after the Second World War. More than 300 000 migrants, mostly from continental Europe, spent time in Bonegilla immediately after their arrival into Australia. This was not a luxurious welcome. Bonegilla was originally established as an army barracks, and it was spartan, at best. Twenty-four blocks, ranged over 600 acres, housed more than 7000 beds. New migrants were placed in communal huts, around a block that had its own kitchen, dining hut, and bath and toilet blocks. Loudspeakers would broadcast instructions. The new migrants would be taught English, ready to staff areas where the country had labour shortages. By the time the Ürges arrived there, in 1957, the camp had been upgraded: huts now had internal walls, lined and painted, and outside, trees had been planted, for shade.

The Ürge family did not have to stay there for long. Les's father's brother had emigrated to Australia after the Second World War, and he arranged work for Les's father at the Port Kembla Steelworks, in the coastal city of Wollongong, south of Sydney. The family joined the many migrants who found their way to the industrial city, then one of the fastest growing in Australia. Between 1947 and 1975, the number of employees at the steelworks swelled from 3665 to more than 20 000, absorbing many of those who had come through Bonegilla.

The sons of these migrant families met on school quadrangles and bonded over football. For the young Les, football was a 'splendid, serene refuge' from the challenges of making his way in his new country.[8] Football also brought the recent arrivals from Hungary together, and helped them create community. For the young Les, football was a passion, and he took this obsession from the schoolyard to television. In the late 1970s, as he began his first job as a football commentator, Laszlo Ürge became Les Murray. Les chose his surname because it meant that he could hold on to his roots: Murray, as he explains in his autobiography, also works as a Hungarian name. For more than three decades, Les Murray worked to make Australians understand this great love. He coined the term 'the world game' to describe the sport, encouraging Australians to take on a vision of football as a truly world game, played beyond Britain. He was tireless in his promotion of soccer to Australian audiences.

I'm here to thank him

In 2011, 55 years after the momentous walk from Pinkamindszent across the border to Austria, Les Murray returned to Hungary. He travelled with his friend and SBS colleague, the journalist Mark Davis. Les was troubled by the discourses around people smugglers in Australia. Since the turn of the new century, refugees and their boats had become a national preoccupation, and opportunistic calls to 'stop the boats' the war cry of successive governments. He wanted to make a documentary, he said, because in the current climate, it had occurred to him that the people smuggler he knew 'was actually a pretty good guy'. Decades after their fleeting encounter, Les remembered how Julius – Gyula – had prevented his father from taking Les's mother's coat. Julius, he told Davis, had 'seemed very honest and sincere, decent'.[9] 'So I'm here,' Les spoke to camera, 'not to arrest him, or even admonish him, but to thank him.'

Les had left Hungary walking through snow, in the dead of winter. He returned to a country enjoying a warm summer, and he looked forward to having a beer with the man to whom he owed his freedom. The documentary accompanied Les as he followed a trail that took him back to Pinkamindszent, and ultimately to surviving members of the Orbàn family. It was only when he reached Pinkamindszent that he discovered that he had arrived three years too late: Gyula had passed away. Gyula's son and grandson were still in the village, running a restaurant, and Les shared that beer with Gyula's grandson, Beles. The two sat together and leafed through a photo album, until Les found the image of the young man he had never forgotten. Gyula never spoke about his activities in the difficult years of 1956–57, and his family knew nothing of it. He never told his son of his own bravery, at a time when the penalty for helping people across the border was death. In Australia, in contrast, Les spoke frequently of Gyula, the people smuggler who helped the Ürge family cross the border into Austria. In his autobiography, in the documentary, and in a short video he made for the Guardian, Murray repeatedly invited Australians to rethink the discourses around people smugglers, with the same passionate energy he had brought to his love of the world game. Gyula, after all, would have been classed as a people smuggler. But Les's memory was of a decent man, who held his and his brother's hands as he led them through a crack in the Iron Curtain. It was this *memory that made Les Murray as tireless an advocate for refugees as he had been for his beloved world game.*

In 1995, Australian band TISM released a song titled 'What Nationality is Les Murray?' 'Is he from Austria?' the song asked; 'Algeria? Bahrain? Bangladesh or Barbados? Bulgaria? Cameroon? Is he from Chad? Chile? China?' In 1995, TISM won the ARIA Award for Best Independent Release. Resplendent in a suit and a highly expressive bow tie, Murray accepted the award on the band's behalf with a few words in Hungarian, in front of a bemused audience. They clapped politely, unaware that they had just been told that the music industry would be the first to go when the revolution came. Les Murray never forgot where he had come from. Nor did he forget the people smuggler who helped him, and his family, to escape danger, and ultimately to come to Australia, to make a new life.

> What nationality is Les Murray?
> Wherefore hails his ancestry?
> Whom does he call the mother country
> When he phones home through OTC?[10]

SILVIE LUSCOMBE: CONNECTIONS

with Julie Kalman

Silvie lives in suburban Melbourne with her husband and twin daughters. She is a university administrator, the sort without whom the department she works in would cease to function, and the building she occupies would cease to stand. It is only the unusual spelling of her name, with an 'i' in place of the usual 'y', and the occasional rich slushiness of Slavic consonants to be heard coming from her office that hint at Silvie's extraordinary history. In early 1980s Czechoslovakia, a lucky connection with a bureaucrat in the Czech regime who was willing to be bribed allowed a young Silvie Hrdlickova, as she then was, to cross the border into Austria on the way to a fictional holiday in Yugoslavia. This was a trip from which her parents Jan and Irena intended never to return.

We were going on a family holiday to Yugoslavia

The excitement was unimaginable to me, a six-year-old being told over a light dinner that we were going on a family holiday to Yugoslavia. Yugoslavia! Wow! Mind you, I had no idea where this place was, but the fact that it had beaches with white sand was the only part my mind filed away. The other important part of the announcement was not to speak to anyone about it, as it was a surprise. I loved surprises, so I did exactly what Mum and Dad asked. Weeks went by, and nothing really exciting happened. Slowly, I planned which toys I would take with me, as they needed to be worthy of travel. I did not want to take my favourite toy and risk it being ruined. My *Babi* (grandma) would come over to our apartment on a daily basis and a great deal of whispering went on in the kitchen between her and Mum, followed by really long and tight hugs as she was leaving. Dad would spend long hours in the garage taking apart our car and putting it back together again. I spent some evenings with him as he did this. Dad was always tinkering with that car. It was something he both enjoyed and was good at, so his activities were nothing out of the ordinary.

In January 1968, Alexander Dubcek had become First Secretary of the Czechoslovak Communist Party. Within weeks of taking office, he had begun to liberalise, easing censorship control of newspapers and broadcasts, and allowing dissidents to raise their voice, without fear of reprisal. For Dubcek, this was his political program, labelled 'socialism with a human face'. It came to be known as the Prague Spring. For authorities in Moscow, however, Dubcek's reforms were cold winds of counter-revolution. Moscow was alarmed by events in Czechoslovakia, and the possible loss of a Cold War satellite. In the late twilight of a European summer night in 1968, tanks rolled through the cobbled streets of Prague, the Czechoslovak capital. On 20 August, Czechoslovakia was invaded by a combined army of Soviet, Hungarian, Polish, East German and Bulgarian forces, dispatched by the Soviet leader, Leonid Brezhnev. Dubcek's reforms were rescinded. New hard-line rulers in the Czech Communist Party clamped down on society with a program called 'Normalisation'. In the great tradition of absolutist regimes, this, of course, was a euphemism. Behind it was a rapid return to highly centralised control of the economy and security, as well as the removal of leading reformers and their supporters, and the reimposition of broad censorship.

Censorship reached into every corner of society. After Silvie was born, in 1975, it hit Jan and Irena hard. Silvie had been seen looking at the stained-glass windows of a church near her home, and she was reported for practising religion. Her parents were taken by police to be questioned. Jan and Irena were also worried for Silvie's future. In order for her to attend university, they would have to 'donate' funds to her teachers. People would hand over their car keys as payment for services such as education, and hospital and dental care. Jan and Irena decided to leave their home in Brno, in the southeast of today's Czech Republic, and defect to the West. They had friends whose siblings had emigrated to Australia, and they decided that this would be their destination.

The last time I saw him

The day of our holiday finally arrived! My *Babi* came to our apartment first thing in the morning to bid us farewell. There were tears. My grandfather, who lived in the same building, waved to us from his window but didn't come down to say goodbye. This was the last time I saw him before he passed away, something that I regret to this day. I always think back to that morning, and all the things that as a child I did not comprehend. I did not know that we were never coming back to the country that was home.

Yugoslavia, with its lovely coastline, was a popular holiday destination for people living in the Eastern Bloc. Czechs travelling to Yugoslavia could cross through either Austria or Hungary on the way. Of course crossing into Austria meant passing through the Iron Curtain, and, as a general rule, this was not allowed. Solidly built checkpoints, manned by soldiers, stood as deterrents. At this time, any movement was very strictly controlled. Anyone wishing to travel, whether within the Eastern Bloc, or from the Eastern Bloc to the West, had to apply for a passport, which had to be given back to authorities shortly after the traveller's return. Only the very privileged were able to keep a passport at home. Family members travelling together would be listed on the same document, but it was a policy of Communist regimes in the Eastern Bloc never to allow an entire family to go away together. One family member always had to remain behind as a sort of hostage, a policy ensuring that the rest of the family would return. Jan and Irena knew that some families had left a child behind and defected, hoping to be able to get the remaining child out of Czechoslovakia later. They almost always failed, and many of them returned. Jan and Irena decided that this was not a risk worth taking. They were lucky to have the luxury of making this decision, but they had access to other means. Silvie's grandmother's partner had contacts in the Communist regime. He was able to obtain a precious piece of paper, on which it stated that the Hrdlicka family had permission to cross into Austria on their way to Yugoslavia. They would have to take the longer route via Hungary on the way back. But Jan and Irena did not intend to return.

We will not be able to go back

The drive to Austria was quiet; no one spoke. I was sitting in the back of Dad's Skoda with a watermelon on the seat next to me. Things were slow at the Czech–Austrian border, as the soldiers would check each vehicle for other occupants that may have been smuggled out of the country. We had a relatively easy crossing, as our passports were all in order and the only comment made by the guards was the fact that we had a watermelon. As we were let into Austria the first thing that struck me was the colour. All the houses were painted a different shade of the rainbow. It was simply beautiful, especially compared to the grey-and-brown concrete architecture that I was used to. My other first memory of Austria was the local corner store where we stopped and bought one raspberry yoghurt and three bananas. This was significant as the only flavour of yoghurt I had ever tasted was vanilla and it was the middle of summer, therefore bananas should not have been available. In Czechoslovakia around Christmas time each family received a ticket that allowed you to purchase one kilo of bananas, a tin of ham (my dad had severe food poisoning from consuming the ham one year) a tin of pineapple and some oranges.

These were imported from Cuba and only available once a year. Now we were having bananas in the middle of summer. Amazing.

We kept driving for another hour, and then my mum and dad stopped the car and just sat for a moment. I thought we had arrived at the beach, and I was eager to get out of the car to look at our holiday spot. But this was not the case. Instead we were parked near a large peeling billboard next to an open wheat field. I listened to my parents saying over and over: 'Should we do this? We will not be able to go back.' Then my dad got out of the car, removed one of the roof racks and rolled out a wad of money, hopped back in the car and drove on in complete silence.

Jan had spent months preparing the car for the journey. As part of the charade, the family had only been able to pack to go on holiday. Too much luggage would have raised suspicion. Their precious laissez-passer, issued by a corruptible bureaucrat, got them to the border. But there, the guards spent a long time examining the car. People regularly tried to defect by creating hiding places. The guards checked the undercarriage with mirrors, they opened the boot and bonnet and went through both with care, and they checked the bench seat in the back of the car, in case a secret hollow had been created underneath. The many hours that Jan had spent mucking about with the car's engine had in fact been to a specific end. The Hrdlickas had left Brno with a different sort of illegal cargo. Any part of the engine that had a hollow, and through which nothing needed to flow, was stuffed with rolled-up notes, equal to 100 koruna, the Czech currency. Jan hid notes in the piping of the roof rack as well – they hadn't been able to sell any of their belongings before leaving, for fear of discovery, but they took whatever they had. They had some extra cash, given by Czech authorities to citizens travelling through other countries, for food and petrol. This is what paid for the yoghurt and bananas that Silvie remembers.

However long the guards took in their inspection felt a great deal longer for the two adult occupants of the car. Eventually they were allowed to pass, and they made their way to Traiskirchen, a former Imperial Artillery Cadet School that had become a stopping point for refugees from the East.

Other families were not so lucky

It was late before we got to Traiskirchen. I don't remember much of what happened next; it is all a bit of a blur. We were ushered into a room, where we were fingerprinted, my parents were interrogated, and then we were assigned a room. I do remember our room as it slept eight people, and there was already a Romanian family in there with their four children. I did not know a single family back home who would have that many children. Language must have been a barrier for the parents to communicate, but us kids just got on. It didn't matter that we didn't speak the same language, children's games were universal and I had a great time.

I remember my dad coming back to the room the second night we were there. He was almost in tears. He spoke to Mum about how lucky we were and how easy our journey had been so far. Then he asked if he could give some people a towel. Years later I asked my mother about the significance of the towel. It turns out when we left Czechoslovakia, we were allowed to do so because we had government permission to cross through Austria. My grandma's partner had used his contacts to obtain this for us. We simply packed for a holiday, drove our car across the checkpoint and arrived in Traiskirchen.

Other families were not so lucky. My dad met another Czech father and his son in the bathroom. The man was using one of his shirts to dry his son, as this was all that they had. Their journey getting into Austria had been tough. They had inflated a rubber dinghy and paddled across a border river in the middle of the night, telling their child that they were playing a game, even as the border guards were shooting at them. We had plenty of towels, and it was the only way we could help, a simple gesture that created a lasting memory. I also remember seeing two men walk past me in the corridor, wearing wingsuits, one orange, and the other green. They, too, had been successful in flying over the border, and were now on their way to be processed.

None of these encounters were quite as memorable as the two Albanian women who became our new roommates. Our Romanian family had moved on, and the room was now empty. One evening, as we made our way back from dinner, there was a commotion outside our door, and two women walked in. These two women were covered in layers of dirt, their cheeks were gaunt and they had the most haunted look about them. Dinner had already been served, and the place did not make any exceptions. Once again, my parents stepped up and offered them some bread and smoked goods we had, just so they could have a meal that night. These poor women had escaped Albania on horseback. Their horses had died halfway through their journey from exhaustion and they had been hitchhiking only at night for weeks. They were just happy to have some stale bread, salami and broken conversation. What makes this story extraordinary was that their friends arrived at the centre the next day, and stood outside the centre passing packages through the bars. That night we didn't have dinner in the hall with the rest of the residents but shared bread, sardines and tomatoes with the most kind-hearted women I have ever met.

Traiskirchen is located 20 kilometres south of Vienna and remains one of the largest refugee centres in the EU. Its refugee camp, known as the Bundesbetreuungsstelle für Asylwerber (Federal Agency for Asylum Seekers), now contains some of the thousands of people who have recently made their way to Europe across the Mediterranean. It was first used to house Hungarian refugees who fled in 1956 after the Hungarian

Revolution. It continued to function as a refugee camp throughout the 1970s and 1980s, mainly for Eastern European refugees but also for refugees from countries in Africa, the Middle East and South America. In 2015, following the recent Syrian crisis, more than 4500 refugees were accommodated there. Amnesty International inspected the centre and found that its living conditions were inhumane and unworthy of human habitation.

To return would mean two years in prison for both my parents

Two weeks passed and we were allowed to leave Traiskirchen to go to Santa Maria, a hotel set up for Czechoslovakian refugees. I will always cherish my time at Santa Maria. At seven, this was the best time of my life. Not a day went by where I didn't explore the river, pick berries in the forests, and visit another hotel down the road. It was magical. It was less magical for my parents. Most dinnertimes would see many of the hotel residents outside calling my name. Some days I would be locked in our upstairs room to ensure I wouldn't be late. My dad managed to get a job as a cobbler, a huge change from the work he had done in Czechoslovakia as an industrial engineer, but it allowed us to have a small income. Meanwhile, over the next six months I continued with my adventures.

My dad's parents were not happy with us leaving, and there were a great many arguments over the phone, but we didn't have the option of going back. To return would mean two years in prison for both my parents. There was a family at the hotel that did go back, they had struggled with being cut off from their loved ones. We never found out what happened to them.

Do we stay in Austria but never really belong, or do we move elsewhere? My parents could have stayed in Austria, but felt they would always be foreigners there. They wanted to leave. Our options were Canada, New Zealand or Australia. Canada would have been our first choice but we would have found ourselves in Montreal, in French-speaking Quebec. It was hard enough to have to learn English, without being burdened with learning French as well. New Zealand was intriguing, but we didn't know anyone in the country and many refugees were sent to the South Island where, aside from farming, work was scarce. Australia it was. While other kids had to go to school, my parents didn't bother enrolling me as we would be leaving soon. As I said, best time ever.

About 6000 Czech refugees arrived in Australia after 1968 on chartered flights from Vienna, continuing a pattern of Austria as a staging post for refugees from Eastern Europe to Australia dating back to post–Second World War. By 1971, they brought the Czechoslovakian-born population in Victoria to 5256. Once they were accepted for settlement in Australia, Jan and Irena had to choose their final destination. One of the cities on the list was Melbourne, and they chose it. The family of Jan's closest friend in Czechoslovakia lived there.

All of the Czechoslovaks who chose Melbourne came to the Maribyrnong Migrants Hostel, northwest of Melbourne. This had been the pyrotechnic division of the Maribyrnong Ordnance Factory, established during the Second World War, to produce fuses, flares and grenades. It closed at the end of the war, and the buildings were immediately requisitioned to house migrants coming to Australia after the war. Australia was unique in this sense. While many countries received displaced people in the wake of the Second World War, only in Australia were they expected to spend their first months in the country in a temporary reception and accommodation facility.

Maribyrnong was typical: located on what was then an urban fringe of the city, in a repurposed building hastily converted, with conditions rudimentary, at best. This was not a welcoming gesture, so much as an opportunity to train these new Australians in the local way of life, and to insulate the housing market, which was stretched to breaking point in the post-war era. By the time Silvie and her family reached Maribyrnong in 1983, the centre had been thoroughly upgraded, and standards of housing were vastly improved. Now, instead of the ex-army tunnel-shaped tin huts that were a feature of life at Maribyrnong, families could live in their own fully furnished flat, with internal toilet and shower. A divan, wardrobes, dressing table, and children's bed and desk were all built in.

For Silvie, who celebrated her eighth birthday in the hostel, life there was fun. Somewhere in her shed at home is the treasured Barbie doll she was given as a present, the first one she had ever seen. In the dusty open spaces, in the looming heat of a Melbourne spring, all of the migrant children found one another. They would gather again in the communal mess hall each evening for dinner. Once a week, the Salvation Army would bring secondhand clothes, and Silvie remembers seeing the bounty spread out for the migrants to take what they might need. Families could stay six months, and this was exactly the length of time that the Hrdlicka family stayed in Maribyrnong. They would have been given help to find the flat that eventually became their home in another part of the suburban fringe.[1]

I wouldn't change a thing

I don't remember much of the flight to Australia. Where we boarded our flight, how long it took or what we saw. I do remember knowing one word and that was 'thank you'. This was used only once on the Qantas flight where I drew the Qantas symbol. With that the attendant came past, pointed at my drawing and said 'kangaroo'. I replied with a 'thank you', and that is all I remember of the entire flight.

From the airport, we were taken to Maribyrnong, which was then a migrant hostel for new arrivals, and there life went back to normal. No more adventures for me. It was back to school, learning English and exploring strange food. I still laugh at the horror of tasting pineapple on pizza, eating Rice Bubbles, or having white-bread sandwiches in packed lunches. Maribyrnong felt like a blip in time. On the one hand, it seemed like we were there for a great deal of time, but on the other, it felt like we were leaving too soon. Soon we moved to Clayton in Victoria, as my dad got a job in Dandenong working for a German engineering company as a fitter and turner. Our unit was bare, and it took weeks to get furniture. You don't realise how much you miss a chair until you have to eat all your meals sitting on the floor. But we had made it. From a rich family life in Czechoslovakia (now the Czech Republic) to nothing (no family or friends) and then again to building a life full of security and peace. We are all happy. Sometimes I wonder what my life would have been like if we had never left. What I would have studied, what opportunities would have been made available? But I look at my husband and children and I know that life is good – no, great – and I wouldn't change a thing.

It was when the family moved to Clayton that Silvie first started school in Australia. She found it strange not to have to change into slippers at the beginning of each day as she entered the classroom. And she was found strange, too, of course. One teacher in particular could not understand why Silvie, who was still learning English, would not respond when spoken to. But foreignness is relative, and as Silvie arrived at Westall Primary School, so, too, did Vietnamese children, fleeing conflict.

Silvie and her parents have all returned to what is now the Czech Republic, more than once, to see family they left behind. Silvie plans to take her daughters soon, too. It is highly unlikely that the anonymous functionary who produced the piece of paper that changed their lives ever told anyone what he had done. His actions were illegal, and the punishment, in Communist Czechoslovakia, would have been stringent.

Unlike Les Murray, Silvie will never have the chance to thank him, or his descendants. But she will not forget the value of that illegally produced document in extreme circumstances.

5

PHUNG: A LEAF IN THE OCEAN

with Nathalie Huynh Chau Nguyen

Phung and I had agreed to meet at her cake shop at the end of the working day on a Thursday. I waited while she finished cleaning the back of her shop and got orders ready for the next day. I remember the steel baking trolleys in her kitchen. She was generous with her time and kindly gave me a piece of cake to take home when we finished the interview in the evening. It would have been a long day for her.

The fall of Saigon on 30 April 1975 marked the end of the Vietnam War and the prelude to one of the largest and most visible diasporas of the late twentieth century in which more than two million Vietnamese left their homeland. Estimates of the number of refugees who died at sea while attempting to escape from Vietnam range from 100 000 to more than one million.[1] The plight of boat people received widespread coverage. Refugees died of thirst or starvation, drowned, or were raped or killed by pirates. The international response to the Vietnamese exodus was unprecedented, involving two major United Nations conferences in 1979 and 1989, and an extensive migration and resettlement program that ended with the closure of the last refugee camp in Hong Kong in 2000. The main countries of resettlement were the United States of America, Australia, Canada and France with Vietnamese resettled in 50 countries worldwide.

The Vietnamese exodus was driven by widespread state repression in post-war Communist Vietnam. One million people were interned in re-education camps (also known as the 'Bamboo Gulag') while another million were forcibly de-urbanised and displaced to New Economic

Zones in rural areas.[2] Freedom of speech and movement was restricted, commerce and agriculture nationalised, and the Vietnamese state discriminated against three specific groups in society: civil and military personnel associated with the former South Vietnamese Government, ethnic Chinese, and Amerasians. Social and familial networks were disrupted as relatives disappeared into the gulag, the New Economic Zones, or as escapees. Phung's father reported for re-education believing that he would see his family again in ten days. Instead he spent five years in the gulag and was sent to re-education camps in central and northern Vietnam, including the far north close to the Chinese border.

We knew the Communists were coming

As a policeman, my father moved around to a lot of different places in central Vietnam but when I was two, our family settled in Vung Tau, and I spent nearly my whole young life there. We had a farm with some livestock, two pigs, four dogs, two geese and some chickens. Vung Tau was a small city. It had a beach, and was calm and peaceful. We heard about the war through newspapers, and we sometimes heard cannons from far away but I didn't really see the suffering of the war. I am the youngest in the family, and I have two brothers and two sisters. Even though my father and mother were poor, they tried to provide us with a comfortable life. But the year I was born, 1963, was the end of the First Republic in South Vietnam, and the war increased from then on until South Vietnam collapsed in 1975. I was 12 years old. The collapse was terrible. I still remember that for three days before the 30th of April we could hear the cannons. We knew the Communists were coming. They destroyed nearly the whole village. I knew that my life had turned another page. We didn't leave Vietnam at the time because my brother was stuck in Saigon, and my parents didn't want to leave without him, so the whole family was trapped in Vietnam.

We believed the Communists when they said that people just needed to go to re-education for ten days. My father didn't go for ten days but for five years and 20 days. At first, he was interned nearby, but then he was sent to central Vietnam, and then to northern Vietnam, and then to the far north and the border between Vietnam and China. A lot of prisoners passed away from hunger, cold and sickness. When, after more than five years, my father returned, he was very thin. His fingernails were as transparent as prawn shells. I was about 17 years old, and I could lift him up easily. My mother sold our furniture so that we could have money to buy food. She tried to buy and sell goods to provide for us but all these activities were illegal so she had to hide the goods in different places. She even cut down her *ao dai* (traditional Vietnamese tunics) to make clothes for my sisters and me.

Life was really difficult after the war. We were starving because we had no rice. When my mum cooked food, she would cook one part rice, and two or three parts potato or corn. I hated it but we had no choice.

My older brother became a medical student in 1974, but after 1975 he had to leave the university and work on the farm. My sister could not get a job. My other brother failed his school exams because my father was a re-education camp prisoner. If you were from a Communist family, you would pass even if you were a bad student. If you were from a Republican family, you would fail even if you were a good student. So my brother had to quit school and become a cyclo driver. I was able to stay in school until Year 12 but I failed my university entrance exam for the same reason: I was from the wrong background.

Phung witnessed the deaths that resulted when people tried to use semi-official escape routes to leave the country. In 1978–1979, the Vietnamese Government collaborated with overseas crime syndicates *to organise boat departures, and charged refugees US$2000–3000 for Government-sponsored escapes.*[3] *The Vietnamese state could thus dispose of any undesirables in the new political order and seize any property or assets left behind by departing refugees. In the case of the* Huey Fong *cargo ship, for example, which arrived in Hong Kong on 23 December 1978 with 3318 refugees on board, the Vietnamese Government 'stood to make £2 million from this "consignment", over and above the confiscation of property and other exactions'.*[4] *Government-sponsored escapes were organised through the Public Security Bureau, with '50 per cent of the proceeds for the government, 40 per cent for the boat, fuel and provisions, [and] 10 per cent left for the boat owner and organizer'.*[5] *This semi-official means of escape was supposed to be safer, but for many it became a 'one-way ticket to a watery grave'.*[6] *The Vietnamese Government facilitated the movement of refugees for its own policy ends in what amounted to a form of 'state-sanctioned expulsion'.*[7]

Phung's memory of the washed-up bodies of those who had opted for Government-sponsored escapes has always haunted her, especially because she recognised people she had known, including her classmates.

I lost a lot of friends

A lot of my friends tried to leave Vietnam. I lost a lot of friends because their escape failed. The government was terrible. If the boat could load 100 people, they would load 200 or 300 people, so when the boat sank more people died. The government cheated them, they said they would let them go but at the last minute, they destroyed their boats and their engines, that's why the next day I would go to the beach and find the bodies of my friends washed up on the shore. I saw some of my classmates and some babies. I couldn't eat when I got home because I felt so terrible. I saw bodies nearly every week, and a lot of people were sent to jail.

I saw the bodies of more women and children than men because women didn't know how to swim. A lot of women and children went by themselves because the fathers were interned. A lot of fathers advised the women to escape from Vietnam with their children. The fathers in jail felt terrible because they couldn't do anything and didn't know when they could return to their families. That's why they advised their wives not to wait for them.

When the government allowed the Chinese people to leave from 1978, they did so because they wanted to collect the gold from the Chinese. A lot of people who wanted to leave changed their names to Chinese surnames. At that time my sister worked in a local hotel. The Chinese who wanted to escape from Vietnam needed to stay there and wait a day for the government to let them go. My sister saw terrible things such as the government letting people go in stormy weather. There would be 200 people in the morning, and in the evening only 100 people would be back. My sister did not know whether the remaining 100 had drowned or been taken away and interned. It was a terrible time.

Phung's family organised their own escape and left in a small boat, although they did charge a small fee to four family friends to be included on their cross-border journey.

Phung's family were fortunate because many boat escapes were unsuccessful. The Vietnamese state did not appear to have a set policy relating to failed escapees. Boat people who were caught by the Vietnamese authorities were either fined if they were lucky or interned for periods stretching from a few months to more than a year.[8] Children were interned with their parents, and there were re-education camps reserved for women and children.[9]

Uncertainty about the consequences of failure was one of several factors which made the process of escape fraught. Unless they were fortunate in having either a close relative or friend organising the escape, refugees had to negotiate a fee with people smugglers and hope that they made it successfully through the successive stages of the escape process. Most escapes involved refugees making their way to meeting points, from one means of transport to another, from a small boat to a larger boat, with failure or arrest by the Vietnamese authorities a possibility at each of these stages. Even after refugees made it to the final boat, they could be chased or shot at by Vietnamese patrol boats. Many refugees did not even reach the sea, and drowned in inland rivers. Vietnamese living in riverine and coastal communities in southern Vietnam remember seeing countless corpses floating along the river or washed up on riverbanks or beaches in the post-war years. [10]

We tried to organise one little boat

We waited until my father returned and we tried to organise one little boat for our family. My boat had 22 people but four people were family friends because my mum needed the money. We let them come with us for a cheap price so we could get some more money. But we needed to split my family into two because if we were unsuccessful nobody could help us. So my father and me, one brother and one sister, plus our fiancés went first, then after a year my mum and my other brother and sister left.

My sister saw the Communists put my mum in jail because they wanted to get our house. When I landed in Malaysia I heard about that and I felt so sad. The Communists kicked my mum out and took over our home. My sister had a six-month-old baby, and they told her that she had to move out of the house overnight. She said she couldn't stop her tears because she had to arrange everything. Our neighbours were good people and tried to help. They offered to keep things for our family. My mum was in jail for nine months. She was only able to get out because we sent money under the table to the authorities, otherwise she would have been there longer.

While Phung's family effectively smuggled themselves out of Vietnam, in many other accounts by Vietnamese refugee women, the part played by people smugglers is referred to sparingly and implied rather than stated. The escape from Vietnam constitutes one part of larger life narratives encompassing the women's lives before and after migration. Details relating to the people smugglers and the smuggling process in turn constitute but one part of the escape story. Women's narratives reveal that the journey itself left a clear imprint in their memory while the mechanics of the escape left a fainter trace. Phung, for example, relates that her family 'tried to organise one little boat' but provides no details about who did this, how they went about it, and how long the process took. The stress and anxiety surrounding life after the war, the decision to escape, and the heightened levels of fear and distress during the escape itself loom much larger in women's memories.

We were like a leaf in the ocean

Our escape by boat was alright. A lot of other people had trouble because they didn't have their own boat, and needed to rely on somebody else. In the case of my family, we were just a small group, and our boat was quite small. In the middle of the ocean, I felt that we were in a really small boat. The waves lifted us up and down, we were like a leaf in the ocean but because my brother could control the boat, we did not sink. We did not really starve because my dad knew how to save food, and luckily for us when we neared Malaysia, we saw a fishing boat. They were good fishermen, not bad ones, because they gave us water. After five and a half days, we arrived at Terengganu in Malaysia. They sent us to Pulau Bidong.

People smuggling in Vietnam fell into three broad categories. At one end of the spectrum, families organised small-scale escapes in which they smuggled themselves out of Vietnam. As was the case with Phung's family, they could charge a modest fee to include a few family friends on their cross-border journey, and their actions in that regard would fall closer to humanitarianism rather than smuggling for material benefit.

Most escapes from Vietnam, however, were organised through smuggling networks. These were local clandestine networks revolving around small-scale entrepreneurs who may have decided to assist potential escapees for a number of reasons. Financial benefit would no doubt have constituted a major motive but smugglers also provided refugees with the means to escape from Vietnam, and those who captained the boats effectively became refugees as well. Unless families owned a boat or could obtain one and knew how to sail it, their only option was to resort to people smugglers. Those who were lucky would succeed on their first try but for many others, the process of escape was a record of repeated failures before refugees finally managed a successful departure.

As for semi-official departures organised by the Vietnamese state in collaboration with criminal syndicates at the other end of the spectrum, the aim 'was to flush out Vietnam's 1.2 million ethnic Chinese, to obtain substantial amounts of gold and foreign currency and to guarantee the refugees a safe passage, a worthless guarantee in light of subsequent events and the dilapidated conditions of the ships'.[11]

Phung's escape with her family members differed in scale from larger escapes organised by local smuggling networks or by the Vietnamese Government. In all three categories, however, the refugees' situation was precarious, and the margin between survival and death narrow. Phung's account attests to the level of desperation and the strength of will that drove people to escape. She witnessed the consequences of failed escapes, and recognised people she knew among the bodies washed ashore, and yet she still made the journey with her family in a small boat.

We thought the airport looked so shiny

We spent a month in Pulau Bidong. Dad was allowed to go to America with us kids but not our mum. He told them that he didn't want that, he wanted the whole family to be reunited. They also told him that he could only bring his single kids with him, without their fiancés. So Dad didn't want to go to America. But Australia said he could bring his whole family with him. So we filled in their application forms and then they interviewed us. I just needed to wait two months at the transit camp in Kuala Lumpur, and I arrived in Australia exactly three months from the day I escaped from Vietnam.

The first day in Australia was very cold. We only had thin summer clothes from Kuala Lumpur and nothing else. When we landed, we thought the airport looked so shiny while we looked like beggars. Luckily, when we arrived at the hostel, we were given some more clothes and food. We stayed at the hostel for three months, then we left and rented a house. After three months, I got married.

I met my fiancé in Vietnam, he was an anaesthetist, and my father offered him a place on the boat with us because he wanted our family to stay together. I think my marriage was wrong because we had been here for too short a time before we got married. The first few years were alright because we tried to build up our family. We had agreed that he would go back to medical school and that I would work to help him but he saw that we could make money by becoming machinists, so he quit his studies and worked instead.

I had a baby at that time so I couldn't go back and study. We were different in our thinking so that's why we split up after nineteen years. When Vietnamese husbands leave their wives, they leave the responsibility for the kids on their wives' shoulders. My husband hasn't provided any support, so I needed to work a lot. Now, it's alright because my kids are growing up: one finished university, the other one nearly so. I still work hard because I want to later retire and then go back to school.

From 1000 people in 1975, the Vietnamese community in Australia has grown to 277 400 people in 2016 or 1.2 per cent of the Australian population. It is the largest refugee community in Australia. There were three main waves of Vietnamese arrivals: the first wave consisted of a small group of 539 well-educated refugees in 1975–1976; the second included many ethnic Chinese escaping from Vietnam after the closure of private businesses in 1978 and the border war between China and Vietnam that same year, with numbers peaking at 12 915 in 1979–1980; and the third consisted largely of so-called 'economic refugees', with numbers peaking at 13 248 in 1990–1991. By 1996, a total of 150 000 Vietnamese had resettled in Australia. Vietnamese refugees formed the first and most difficult test case of the abolition of the White Australia Policy, and received high exposure in the Australian media and in public discourse on the topic of Asian immigration. From the mid-1990s, the number of Vietnamese arriving as refugees declined, with most arriving under family reunion. The Vietnamese in Australia are now a well-established community. The number of migrants from Vietnam to Australia in the 2010s was relatively low and outnumbered by international students and visitors from Vietnam. For example, in 2014–15, there were 5100 permanent migrants from Vietnam, but 10 283 international students, 31 306 tourists and 8674 business visitors from Vietnam.[12]

My old-fashioned ways

I haven't gone back to Vietnam but I still follow the news and read newspapers. I feel sad because it looks colourful on the surface but there is still a lot of poverty in Vietnam. My kids always ask questions about why my generation is like this, and I explained to them that before 1975, we had a good education, and good morals. It is different from people in Vietnam now. Whenever there is a disaster in Vietnam, Vietnamese from all the other countries send money and help but the people in Vietnam don't really help each other and rely on Vietnamese overseas.

I am really happy in Australia. The only thing I need to think about is that there are differences between East and West, and sometimes I need to choose which one is suitable for my kids. Of course, sometimes my kids disagree with me, and we need to compromise. For example, if you go with Australians to a restaurant, you need to split the bill but I prefer the old way of paying once, and you pay the next time. If Asians want to do something for others they offer to help while Australians do not normally offer and wait for you to ask, and then they help you. I prefer to offer to help people rather than wait for them to ask. These are just some examples of my old-fashioned ways.

6

CARINA HOANG:
MY PEOPLE SMUGGLER WAS MY SAVIOUR

with Ruth Balint

The date 30 April 1975 marked the end of the Vietnam War. For Carina and her family, it was the beginning of a new period of oppression and persecution. At 16 years old, with her two younger siblings in her care, she finally joined over a million people fleeing Vietnam who became known to the world as the Vietnamese 'boat people'.

My father was the Chief of a Military Police Department in a province south of Saigon. He was captured by the Communists on 29 April 1975 and incarcerated for more than 13 years, joining hundreds of thousands of people associated with the Government of South Vietnam or the United States of America, kept in prisons that were commonly referred to as 're-education camps'. He never had a trial or a sentence.

For 13 years, we did not know if he was going to be released. While he was imprisoned, our family, like many others, also faced persecution. All the money from my parents' bank account was seized. Our house was confiscated. The government also appropriated my mother's factory. After that, my mother was unable to get a job due to our father's military background.

Every few months my mother had to bribe the local authorities so that we could stay in our own town and avoid being sent to the New Economic Zones (NEZs) in a remote rural area. NEZs were ridden with mosquitoes and poisonous snakes, and lacking in shelter, drinking water, food and sanitation. Facilities for healthcare, education and communication were non-existent. Life was extremely difficult in those zones for people who were not conditioned to hard labour. Death rates were high, particularly among children and the elderly. Those who escaped were penalised by jail terms and then returned to NEZs.

My mother began to arrange
for her children to escape

My mother struggled to raise seven children and look after her mother and mother-in-law while hanging on to the hope that someday my father would be released from prison. In late 1978, when Vietnam launched a full-scale invasion of Cambodia, she worried about her children being sent to war, and began to arrange for her children to escape. First to go were my older sister and younger brother, they were 16 and 14. After she received the news that they had reached a refugee camp in Malaysia, my mother began to organise for me and my other siblings to leave the country. For over a year my two younger siblings and I made three attempts to escape. The first time we were almost caught by the police near the beach in central Vietnam. The other two times we were cheated. People who claimed they had a boat took gold from my mother but the trips never materialised.

Vượt biên (crossing the border) was considered a serious offence. If caught, people who tried to leave Vietnam illegally could face a prison term of up to three years, and up to ten years for the boat owners, the skippers and the organisers. Depending on the region where they began their journey, Vietnamese people used two types of boats to escape. Those who left from southern Vietnam used small fishing boats equipped with engines that might not sustain their journey. Their route began from Vung Tau or the Mekong Delta then across the South China Sea to Southeast Asia. Those who left from northern and central Vietnam crossed the Gulf of Tonkin and followed the coastline to Hong Kong, using primitive, ancient Chinese-designed junks. People who were in the fishing industry left on their own boats. Sometimes, families and friends gathered money to buy a boat and hire a skipper to take them out of the country. Most of the time, the skippers brought their family along. Not only because they wanted their family to leave the country with them, they were also worried that their family would be persecuted if the government found out that they had left the country.

According to the United Nations High Commissioner for Refugees (UNHCR), between 1975 and 1995 a population of 796310 Vietnamese boat people (VBP) arrived in Southeast Asia.[1] On the open seas, they faced severe storms, starvation, dehydration, and many perished at the hands of pirates and leaky boats. It is estimated that around one out of three died during the journey.

The organisers were under increasing pressure to get everyone out

We finally succeeded on our fourth attempt. This time, my mother knew one of the three boat organisers – we called him Uncle Dao. These men were Chinese–Vietnamese and they were business owners in Chinatown. In 1977, Uncle Dao and his two friends got together and planned a trip for themselves, their families and friends to leave Vietnam. They raised money to buy the boat, and obtained tools, fuel, food and water supplies, and hired a skipper. It took them nearly a year to prepare, and then they registered the boat and the passengers with the government.

These people were allowed to 'đi bán chính thức' (leave the country semi-legally) because they were ethnic Chinese. During the late 1970s, the Chinese–Vietnamese experienced increasing official hostility. Growing rivalry between Vietnam and China meant that the Vietnamese Government closed down businesses owned by ethnic Chinese, confiscated their properties and forced them to leave the country or move to NEZs. Subsequently, many thousands of ethnic Chinese left southern Vietnam and 'đi bán chính thức'.

But it wasn't easy. People like Uncle Dao first had to give up their homes and businesses to the government, and then each person had to pay a fee to the authority for the permission to leave, and a fee to the organisers for their trip. While waiting for their departure, they were not allowed to work and had to live off whatever money they had left. A year and a half later, Dao, his friends and their families were still stuck in limbo, because they were unable to obtain the exit permit for the boat from the local authorities. They were running out of money, and circumstances had changed. Older family members had passed away and some children were born. The organisers were under increasing pressure to get everyone out of Vietnam as soon as possible.

Around February 1979, a friend of Uncle Dao introduced him to my mother because she knew someone who could issue the exit permit for the boat. After a few months of negotiations and a lot of money paid under the table, they finally got their exit permit for the boat. During the month of May, the organisers were busy gathering everyone together. It was not an easy task, as many of these people had surrendered their houses to the government and moved away. Often, the families had split up and their members were living in different places. Many of them had left Chinatown: they lived everywhere in and outside of Saigon city. Telephone communication was not an option then. So, the organisers were basically on their motorcycles looking for their 'passengers' to deliver messages about the departure.

Our grandmother's funeral was a blessing

Our grandmother died at the same time we heard the news of the boat's imminent departure. While organising the funeral and carrying out the three-day ritual of greeting family and friends who came to the house to pay respects and light incense at the coffin, my mother and I secretly prepared my journey at night.

After we buried our grandmother, we had to return to the cemetery for the 'open the gate of the tomb' ritual. On that day my mother decided to send me straight to Vung Tau from the cemetery to stay there until the boat left. At the time, very often, local policemen would come to anyone's house at night unannounced, to count the heads of the people who were registered as living there. If there were more or less than the expected number of people present, the head of the household would have a lot to answer for, and the usual consequence was a jail term. But we were lucky. Because of the busy activities of the funeral and the high number of visitors, the local authorities and neighbours would not have noticed my absence. If they had, my mother would have used our grandmother's funeral to explain and hopefully get away with it.

We had fake birth certificates and pretended we were Chinese

At the end of May, more than 370 adults and children were camped at a campground in Vung Tau for several days waiting to get on the boat. Vung Tau is a port city on a peninsula in southern Vietnam, approximately 100 kilometres from Saigon. It was a common place from where Vietnamese boat people departed. My siblings and I joined them. There were several thousand people at the campground also waiting for their departure on other boats. Presumably they were ethnic Chinese. We had fake birth certificates and were pretending we, too, were Chinese. For me, the added risk of using a fake birth certificate and pretending to be ethnic Chinese was getting caught. If I was caught, I would have to spend at least a year in a forced labour camp and joining the war in Cambodia was inevitable. But at the time, my mother and I didn't even consider the consequences, our ultimate goal was for me and my siblings to leave Vietnam.

Buying a fake birth certificate was not difficult, you just needed money and to know who to go to. At the time, all over South Vietnam, there was a large demand for fake certificates, not only for those trying to leave the country like me, but also for those who had lost their paperwork during the chaos of the war. Without some form of identification and proof of origin, people were at greater risk of being sent to the NEZs. The 'twisted' effect of me using the fake birth certificate, which I didn't see coming, was that I was unable to say my last goodbye to my mother. As she was involved in getting the exit permit for the boat, local authorities knew that she was Vietnamese. Hence, I had to be extremely careful not to reveal our relationship.

On the morning of 31 May 1979, we were called to the pier to get on our boat. At the checkpoint, two police officers and the organiser were checking each person against their ID that was registered in the logbook. By the afternoon, the checking process was complete, but the police officers did not allow a group of children to board the boat. Some of them were not registered because they were born during the waiting period. In other cases, when the parents made the registrations, they either did not have to pay a fee for the children who were under five, or they only paid half of the fee if their children were under 12 years old. However, after two years of waiting, some of these children became older than five or over 12, so their fees had changed. Not all of the parents had the gold to pay for the children. Uncle Dao and the other organisers went around to all the passengers and asked them for donations. They collected a big hat full of cash, gold coins and jewellery to give to the police officers in order for the children to be released to their parents.

That evening, my two siblings and I finally left Vietnam on a 25-metre by 4-metre wooden boat, numbered *VT075*. It was common for these ethnic Chinese boats to be packed with three or more times their capacity. Most often, local authorities added a substantial number of people to the boats right before their departure. Refusal was not an option for the boat owners. We were with 370 other people, including Uncle Dao's grandparents who were in their 80s. I was 16. There were many unforgettable moments during my escape journey, but my most bitter and vivid memory was when I crossed the checkpoint to get on the boat. My mother was standing next to the policemen who cross-checked every passenger, the 'boat person', against the logbook. As I walked past her, I looked down trying to hold back my tears, I ground my teeth and clenched my fists. I felt a huge lump of anger in my throat.

Military men fired at our boat

It was a horrendous eight-day journey across the South China Sea. During our first night we were struck by a storm so violent that our boat felt like a cradle being rocked by angry hands. There was an indescribable mixture of sounds as children cried, adults screamed, the thunder roared, and waves crashed on us. Every time it seemed our boat was going to be smashed up, more than 300 Chinese and Vietnamese people, in different dialects and accents, desperately prayed to our various saviours – the Virgin Mary, Jesus, Buddha, ancestors. Never had I felt so vulnerable. For years I used to wake up in the middle of the night to the sound of people chanting in my head. After the storm we were left sitting in a slimy mixture of vomit, urine and seawater. I went around the boat to look for Uncle Dao and asked him to let my siblings and I move to the deck because it was so stuffy and humid where we were sitting.

On the fourth and fifth days, two groups of Thai pirates chased us. All the women and girls were sent to the bottom of the boat, where we smeared soot and rubbish over our faces and bodies to make ourselves as ugly and as smelly as possible, in the hope that the pirates would not want to rape us. Luckily, we got away. Later I was told that, if we'd been caught, what we did would have made no difference. On the evening of the sixth day we were prevented from approaching Malaysia. Military men fired at our boat, then jumped on board and stole our maps, compass and valuables. One of them pointed a gun at my brother's neck and demanded his gold necklace. I thought he was going to shoot my brother. For years after being resettled in the United States, I still had nightmares about that soldier with his rifle. Then they tied our boat to theirs, towed us back out to the South China Sea, fired a few more rounds into the air, cut the rope and left us out there in the dark. By mid-morning of the seventh day we were running out of water and food and had hardly any energy left. Our first casualty was a 70-year-old man who died of hunger and suffocation.

At last, on the eighth day, we reached a small fishing village on Indonesia's Keramut Island, where the organisers and the skipper deliberately sank the boat to improve our chances of disembarking. The villagers must have felt overwhelmed – we outnumbered them three to one. Four days later we were transferred from Keramut to Letung Island. It was a bigger island with a large population, as well as schools, shops, mosques, a medical clinic and government offices. Unfortunately, we were not allowed to stay there. Uncle Dao even offered to pay the local authority to let his family and us (my two siblings and me) stay on Letung Island until we left for resettlement, but he was unsuccessful.

After 12 days we made the long boat ride to Kuku Beach on

Jemaja Island. Excited at the thought that we would soon be placed in a refugee camp, I hardly slept the previous night. But as we approached Kuku Beach we could see no signs of huts or anything that looked like a camp. Only once we got ashore did we realise it was uninhabited. The local Indonesian authorities just left us there without shelter, food, water or medicine.

Night seemed to fall quickly and our group of almost 400 people had no alternative but to settle down on the sand between the ocean and the jungle. After dark there was a thunderstorm that soaked everybody. We shivered until the morning sun began to dry us out. We wondered if there had been a mistake, or whether someone would come back in the morning to take us to a nearby refugee camp. We waited all day, then the next day and the next day. Eventually we realised that we were stranded.

Initially we survived on coconuts, jungle fruit and vegetables, seafood – anything we could find in the jungle or in the ocean. Some villagers from nearby Indonesian islands came around with food that they were prepared to exchange for items such as gold, jewellery or American dollars. Those who did not have any valuables continued to search in the jungle. In order to buy medicine and feed the three of us, I sold the jewellery that my mother had given me and my sister. Before the UNHCR found us three months later, many had died of malnutrition and dehydration, malaria, diarrhoea and other diseases.

My sister, brother and I all contracted malaria. When we were shivery and cold, we had neither blankets nor clothing to keep us warm, and when the fever came there was no relief from the heat of the tropical jungle. We also came down with diarrhoea, and I had to make many trips each day to the beach or up the hill to empty our waste bucket. At this time, we did not have any shelter. Uncle Dao let my brother and sister sleep inside the hut with his grandparents and parents. Everyone tried to survive on the uninhabited island with not much more than the clothes on our backs. Being unaccompanied minors, it gave us great comfort having some adults, like Uncle Dao around.

Unaccompanied children (also called unaccompanied minors) are children who have been separated from both parents and other relatives and are not being cared for by an adult. At least 300 000 unaccompanied children were recorded by 80 countries in 2015 and 2016 combined, a five-fold increase since 2010. While the most recent statistics are not available, the situation is comparable. The international organisation UNICEF estimates that at the end of 2018, there were 31 million children displaced globally.[2] The 2018 figures for Europe record that among unaccompanied children seeking asylum, the most common nationalities were Afghanistan (16 per cent) and Eritrea (10 per cent), followed by the Syrian Arab Republic and Pakistan (7 per cent each), Iraq and Guinea (6 per cent each), as well as Somalia (5 per cent). Unaccompanied refugee children represent one of the world's most vulnerable populations.

We had a wonderful reunion

Almost a year after we arrived in Indonesia, my siblings and I were resettled in the United States. When we arrived in the States, we were under the supervision of a relative who volunteered to be our guardian. There were many support groups available to assist newly arrived refugees to adjust, including government agencies as well as non-profit organisations. Our local church and neighbours were generous and helpful. We were given clothes, home appliances and furniture from the church.

We were immediately enrolled in schools and received full medical care and financial assistance from the government. While our guardian was at work he was able to get help from a social worker who as well as being our interpreter, took us to medical and dental appointments and taught us how to navigate public transport. Our neighbour helped me with English and homework after school. Someone from the church even drove us to visit other Vietnamese families living nearby so we would not feel so isolated.

The support from the government and the kindness and generosity from local people, certainly made our resettlement process less challenging. Nonetheless, coping with cultural differences, the language barrier and unfamiliar territory are always difficult for refugees who in many ways have already suffered prior to their arrival. As an unaccompanied minor, my challenges were compounded with feelings of loneliness, homesickness for my parents and a fear of making decisions on my own. I despaired about being unable to speak or understand English. I was also very worried that I would not do well in school and would disappoint my parents.

Within a short time, the ordeal of escaping Communist Vietnam had drastically changed my life over and over again. At 16 I had assumed the role of my parents to protect my younger sister and brother and take care of them. Ten months later I was in high school in the United States where I faced the usual teenage problems: self-esteem and body image. I felt like an old soul trapped inside a young body.

Ten years after I left my country, my father was released from prison. Forced labour and torture had left him with severe health problems. We applied for our parents and my two youngest sisters to join us in the United States. Four years later they joined us in California. It had been nearly 15 years since we left Vietnam when I finally saw my mother again.

My father had several major operations including open heart surgery soon after he arrived. He kept silent about his life in prison for two decades. I finally got to learn about what he went through during the 14 years he spent in prison. The day after he was captured, he was blindfolded with his hands tied behind his back and was lined up to be executed. For some unknown reason, the shooting stopped after several of his comrades were shot. They spared his life but locked him up. 'They did not shoot me, but I've felt a bullet in my head ever since,' my father said.

Carina completed a BA in Chemistry at Rosemont College in Pennsylvania and an MBA at California State University in Pomona before moving to Australia, where she completed another BA in Gender and Cultural Studies at Murdoch University in Western Australia. She has since completed a PhD on a history of the Vietnamese boat people who went to Hong Kong. Her most recent achievement is playing the character Iris in the ABC TV series The Heights.

In 2007 I migrated to Australia from America to be with my, then, Australian husband. I had very minimal problems with the language and cultural differences hence my resettlement process was very short and simple compared to my previous one in America. Although I did not come to Australia as a refugee, I speak English, I was a professional with postgraduate degrees from a Western country I still felt discriminated against because of my origins. On several occasions the people who discriminated against me were professionals and intelligent people. It is undeniable that discrimination exists in our society. However, I believe that it represents a small portion of the general population. I attributed this discriminatory behaviour to lack of knowledge and the influence of purposefully poor language used by leaders and media against people of non-Anglo backgrounds and refugees.

After a few years of searching, we were finally able to locate Uncle Dao in California. We had a wonderful reunion with him, his family, one of the other organisers, and their families. The more than

40-year friendship with our 'people smugglers' (Uncle Dao and the other boat organisers) is still strong and meaningful. We are grateful to them for the opportunity to get out of Vietnam on their boat and they are grateful to my mother for helping them to get the exit permit for the boat.

7

FROM THE HORSE'S MOUTH

Ngo Minh Hoang with Phuong Ngo

Phuong Ngo is a celebrated visual artist, whose innovative installations and artworks attract international acclaim. This rich photographic essay is based on a 2013 exhibition in Melbourne, called 'My Father: The People Smuggler'. The voice in this chapter belongs to Phuong's father Ngo Minh Hoang, telling his story to his son.

I was born on 10 July 1954: the year of the horse. My date of birth in Australia is the 1st of July 1954 because I couldn't remember the actual date when we arrived in Malaysia in 1981.

When I was in Vietnam I finished the sixth grade, but I couldn't continue. Before the war ended, if you failed the entrance exam for school you would have to join the ARVN (Army of the Republic of Vietnam); I didn't want to do this so I decided to pick up a trade. I wanted to become a mechanic.

I found a ship's mechanic who worked at the docks, and he agreed to take me on as an apprentice with my father's permission. I was 12 or 13 years old.

After two years as an apprentice I went out on my own and became the mechanic for a ship; I did this work right up until 30 April 1975, the day the Communists took over our country. Everything changed under the Communists. My wage at the time was 40 Dong in the new currency, and the conversion rate from the South Vietnamese currency to this new currency was 500 to one.

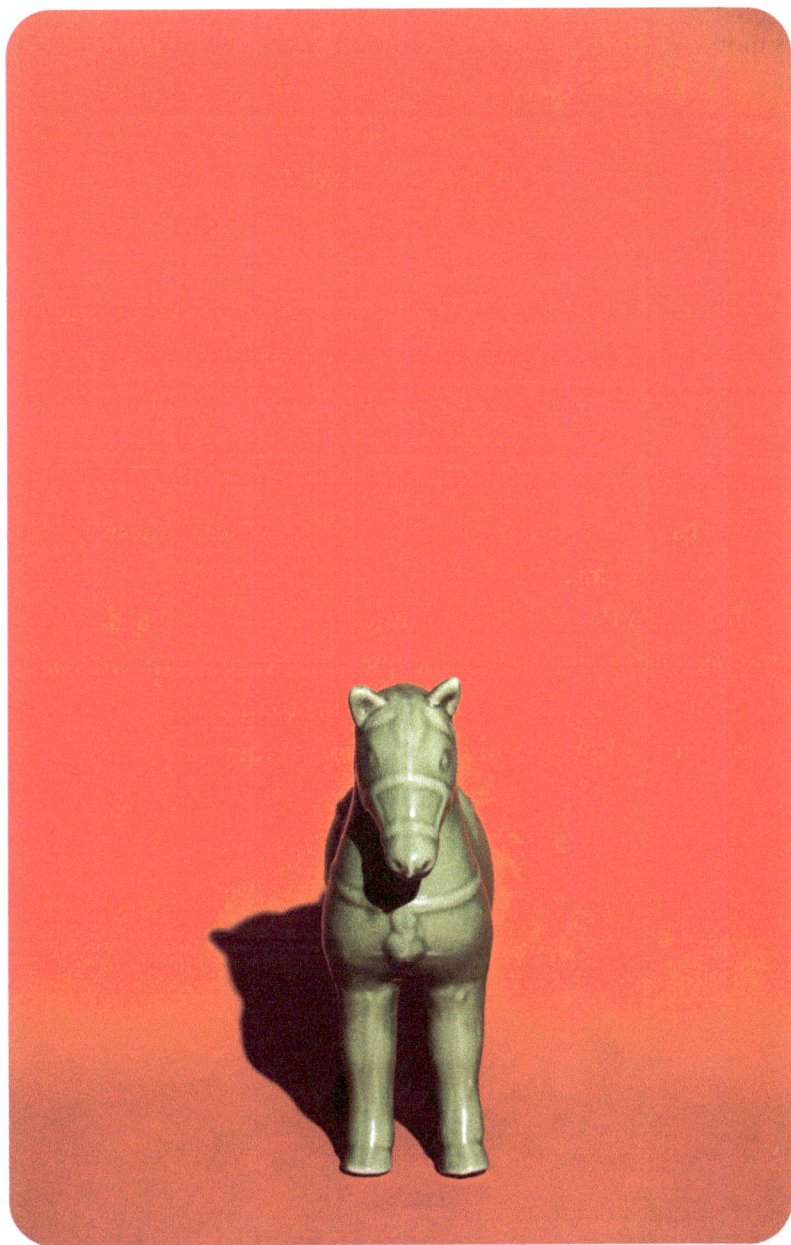

This was probably why your maternal grandfather died. He had all his money in the bank when the war ended, and the conversion rate meant that he lost everything. Back then if you had one billion in South Vietnamese currency, they would exchange it to a few hundred Dong, and relocate you to rural areas in order to implement the new economic regime.

Around August and September of 1977, I became involved with staging escapes. I was assisting someone who noticed that I was a good worker, so they put forward the money for me to organise an escape. From buying the boat and engine, to planning the route through the river systems and the movement of people, I did it all. As a ship's mechanic I had the skills to plan and organise everything, they just gave me the money do it; the method of orchestrating the escape was up to me.

The reason they approached me was because they had failed on a number of occasions. These people were friends with my friends, and at some point had started to invite me to their homes for dinner. They saw me as honest and hardworking so they gave me money to do the job.

On that first trip, we got out to the sea but there was a storm, the winds were strong and the waves were large. I ran the boat fast into the current because I thought that it would get us past the danger of the rough seas, but this was the wrong approach, I should have gone slowly. Because I went in fast the waves pushed us back to shore. We call it dragon water.

There was a small island in the middle of the river through My Thanh, so we had to navigate our way around it to get out initially, and then again on the way back. It was pitch black and I lost my bearings, but I had to lead people into the jungle to hide. It wasn't until sunrise that we realised I had led the passengers into the heart of a re-education camp. The Communists captured us. I was in prison for six months. It was a South Vietnamese prison that was run by the Communists. We were given rice to eat.

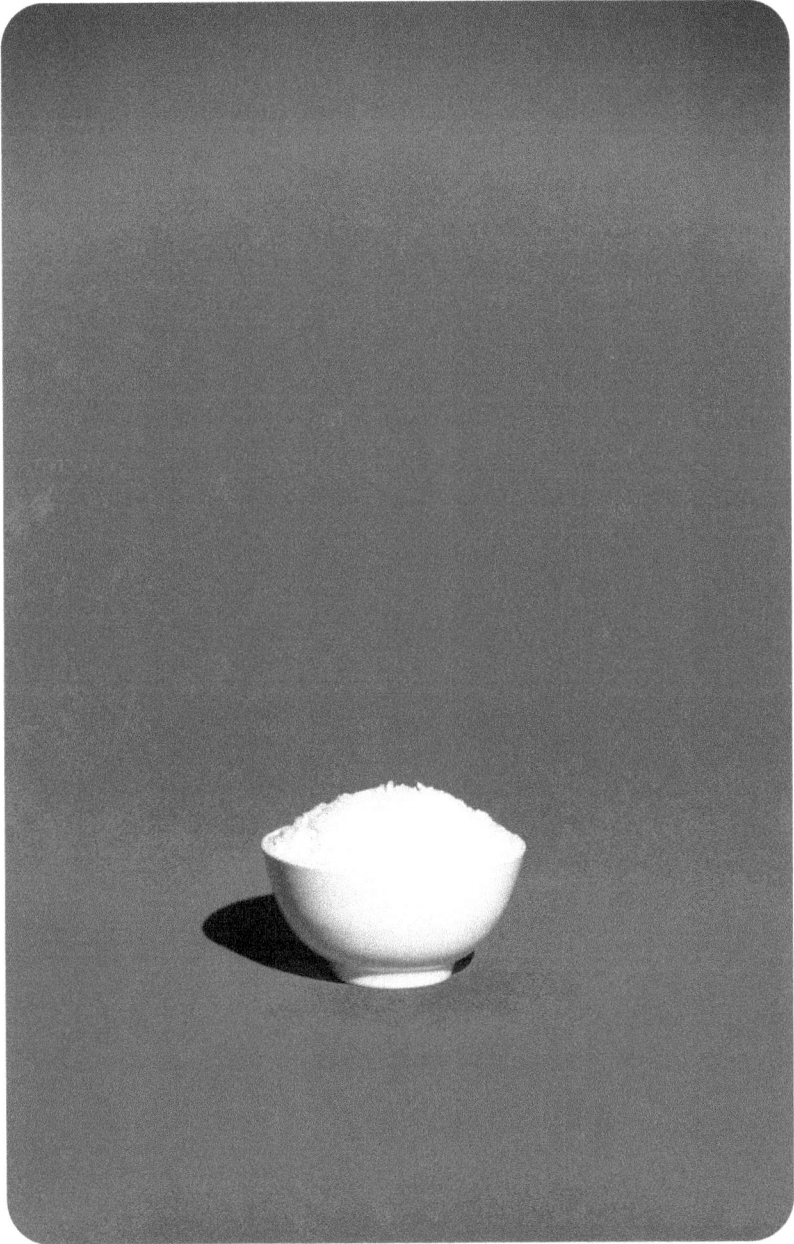

It wasn't proper rice, more like pig slop. The food wasn't great, but given the situation there wasn't much of an expectation.

When I was in prison I had to do hard labour. It wasn't labour for the government. Rather I was working the land for the generals and officers that ran the prison. We would work the land and properties that they seized for themselves following the war.

After six months I left prison. I started working to help people escape the country again, but this was during a time when the government would look the other way, or you could buy your escape from the Communist Government. This would have been 1978 or 1979, when there was conflict with China, and the government wanted to remove the ethnic Chinese population from Vietnam.

At this point my fortunes had changed, because escapes were easier. People wanting to organise boats needed ship mechanics. I organised two to three boats. In 1978 I was 24, these were not my own boats or escapes, I worked as a mechanic, getting boats ready for the Chinese who had an agreement with the government that they could leave the country as boat people. People wanted me to leave with the boats I was working on, but I was making good money, so I decided to stay in Vietnam and continue this work. At that stage I hadn't met your mother yet. If I had left I could have taken seven people with me at no cost, at that time for one person to go they had to pay one tael of gold (1.3 ounces).

Sometimes, after we had paid for the escape and organising the boats, the Communists closed the harbour and raided our vessels, confiscating and stealing property. In one of these instances I had left all my tools and equipment on the boat, I had gone to buy parts and didn't get back in time to collect my stuff and they took it all. They had let the people working on the boats at the time take their tools and equipment, but because I wasn't there they wouldn't let me back on the boat to retrieve my property.

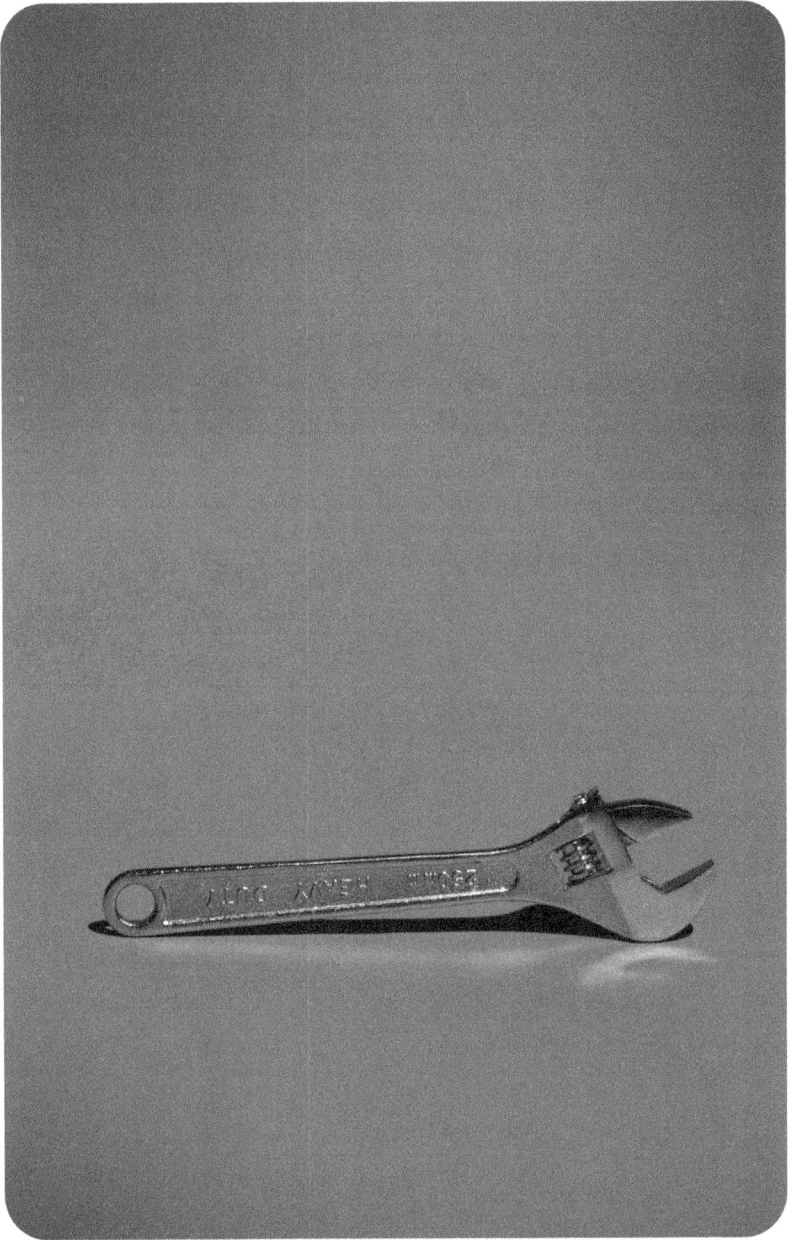

After this period I went to work putting together boats for people who were fleeing, the ones that didn't have formal passage to escape. I did this for a short while, and some people got out while others didn't and ended up in prison. The problem was that I would get the boat to the rendezvous point and we had to wait for people to meet us, but sometimes no one would arrive because they were led the wrong way or were captured. It was from this point that people asked me to coordinate the entirety of these escapes; that is when I started to do everything and I was able to complete four escapes in total. I was successful each time. During these four escapes there were numerous times when we couldn't leave or had to try again, but we were never caught.

Of these boats, two, including the one we were on, ended up in Malaysia. The one your Uncle Seven was on was picked up by a Philippine fishing trawler, but by then four or six people had died on board; they were at sea for 21 days because their engine broke down. Aunt Four's boat landed in Thailand.

Towards the end of this time I met and married your mother. It was 1980, and I was questioning whether I wanted to continue this work. The price to flee at the time was two tael, about 2.5 ounces, sometimes three tael.

After I married your mum, I was almost done with the work, and when your brother was four and a half months old we left on my final boat. It was September 1981, your brother was born on 8 April on the lunar calendar; the date on the Gregorian calendar would have been 11 May. This is why his date of birth here is incorrect.

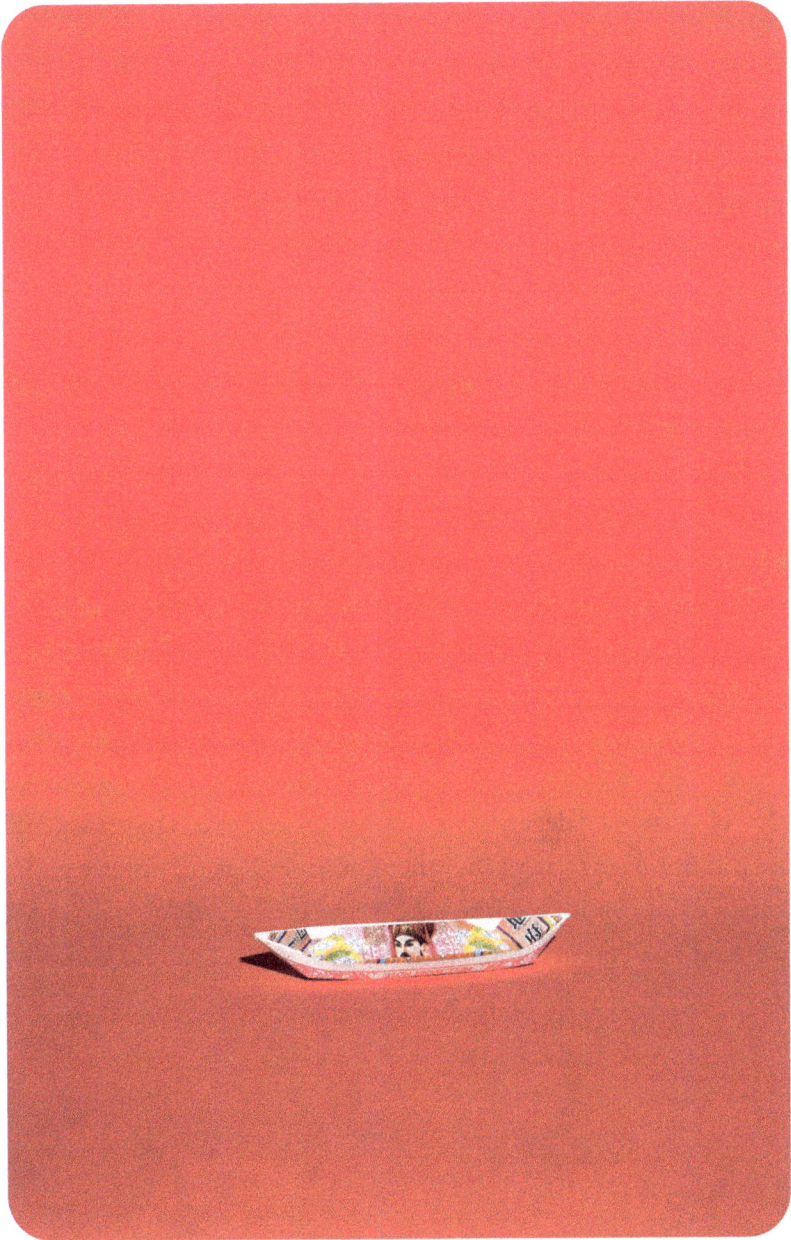

I remember that we arrived at Kuala Terengganu on 28 October and were transferred to Pulau Bidong on 30 October. The first thing I saw from the boat at the end of our journey was the light of Kuala Terengganu. We were at sea for 72 hours and because of this everyone was still in good health. I saw a red light on Terengganu, it was like a television signal tower. The street lights were still too blurry and because we were so far away I could not see them clearly. I steered the boat slowly towards it until the sunrise. When I could see, I ran the boat straight to shore and made sure that whoever had the most strength would take care of your brother and mother. These people were the first to get off the boat; I was the last one to leave because I stayed on board to destroy the engine. This was so that Malay authorities wouldn't push us back out to sea.

When we landed we were each given two boxes of chrysanthemum tea, toothpaste, a toothbrush and towel. We were given the chrysanthemum tea when we got to the processing centre. Each person got two boxes. After this two buses came, and took all 79 passengers to Merang. We were then transferred to Pulau Bidong. A few days later a delegation of Australians came to interview people who did not have relatives in other countries. I had a sister who had escaped to the United States, but I wanted to go to Australia. I told them that I had family who had also escaped, but I had no idea where they were.

Three months after this the Australian delegation came back and advised me that they had located my sister in the United States and asked me if I still wanted to go to Australia. I told them yes, I still wanted to go to Australia. After this I did not hear anything for a while so I went to complain to them. A few weeks after this we were listed to go to Australia.

Before we left the camp we had medical checks and had our photos taken, these are the photos that we still have now. We were leaving in the evening, so that last day in the camp was happy and there was nothing to worry about, so we had photos taken. When we were fleeing Vietnam there were obvious concerns, but leaving the camp we only had bright futures to look forward to, it was a happy time.

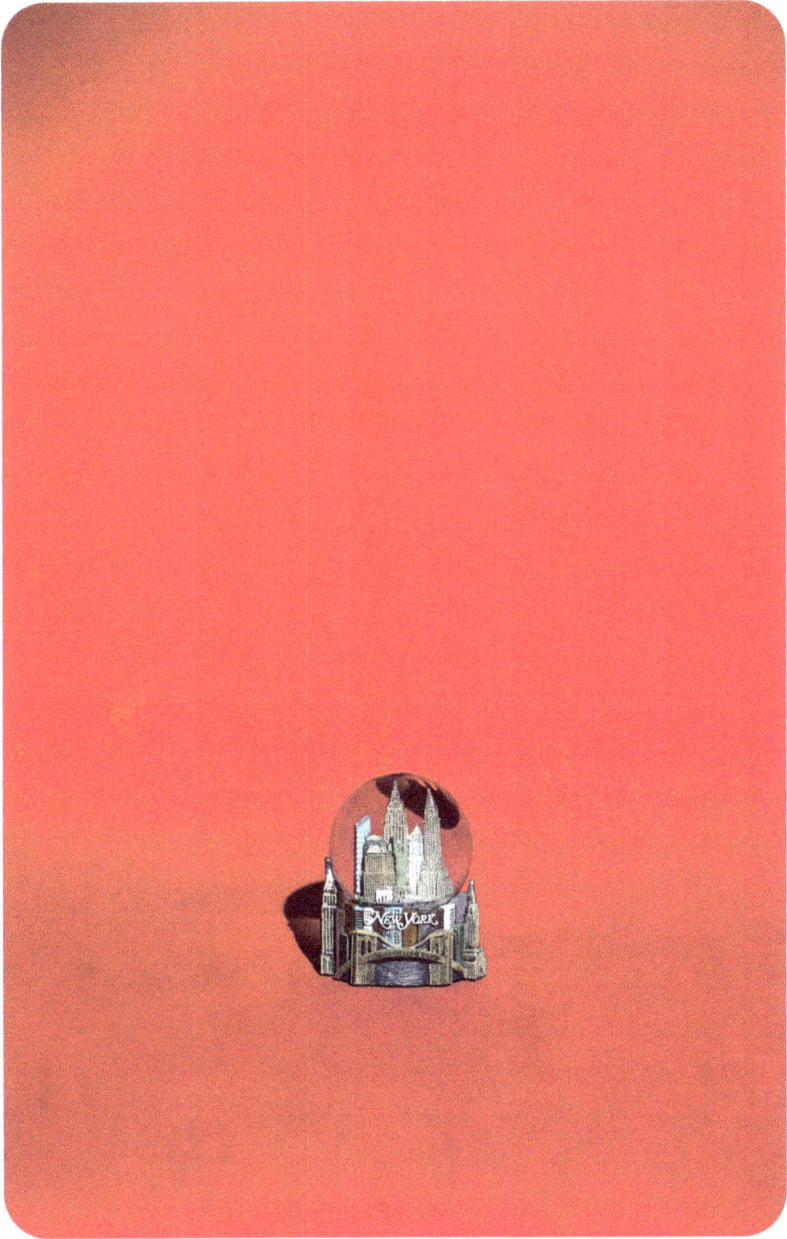

After this we were transferred to a processing centre near Kuala Lumpur where we stayed for a month for health checks. We arrived in Australia on 28 June 1982, your mother, brother, aunt, cousin and myself. Your sister was still in your mother's belly.

I will never forget my first day in Australia, when we landed at Melbourne airport. We had to disembark the plane and get on a bus, but everyone ran back onto the plane. It was 28 June 1982, we had come from our tropical climate since we were born, we had never experienced this kind of bizarre cold. It took all of our will and might to run out of the plane and onto the vehicle, which had heating. We had no idea there would be heating on the bus, we expected it to be just as cold.

We were then taken to Midway Hostel. It was about six or seven in the morning and people were having breakfast. For six or eight months I hadn't had any meat and saw that they had lamb liver, I took a large plate of the liver, took one bite and had to throw it all out. I had no idea that it would smell and taste so bad. I then found bacon and other things that I could eat. When I was in Vietnam I craved liver and enjoyed it, like pork liver, I thought lamb liver would be just as delicious, but it was unpalatable. I will never forget that.

Not long after this, we were taken to Adelaide on a bus. There your sister was born and you were born the year after. We have been here ever since, Adelaide is our home village now.

Leaving Malaysia, 1982
L–R: Tam Ngo, Tien Thai (Mum), Hoang Ngo (Dad),
Phuc Thai and Phong Ngo (brother).

8

MARAMA KUFI: SAVING THE CHILDREN

with Julie Kalman

Marama Kufi is a tall, elegant man in his fifties. He greets me warmly, and we order coffee. Marama was born in 1968 in Ethiopia, a country of more than 90 different nations, nationalities and ethnic groups, each with their own language, way of life, culture and customs. Marama comes from Oromia in the country's west, one of the main regions in today's Ethiopia. He was born into a farming family in the western town of Mendi, and he was one of five children, with two older sisters, and a younger sister and brother. His parents farmed coffee and bred cattle. They were comfortably off, and his parents were well known for the role they played in their region as traditional judges, resolving minor disputes and helping others.

The family belonged to the Ethiopian Orthodox Church, but as children, Marama and his younger brother began to attend Sunday Bible study and choir with others in their social group. Gradually, this extended to Sunday worship, and, ultimately, conversion to Lutheranism. The two brothers attended the Swedish Missionary School, 'the only available close and good school', two hours' walk each way. After he finished school, Marama qualified as a teacher.

They were trying to be children

It was Friday morning. From a distance, the morning sun shone eye-catchingly bright as it rose above the mountain range, the two fitting neatly together. It was autumn; the weather was glorious, and the soft and relaxing wind fed people's spirits.

The schoolyard was full of students. Before the start of class, they were playing in the playground, dividing up into groups by their age and gender. They were all busy. Everyone had something to do. Some were running around and chasing each other. Others were digging in the soil or chasing a ball, or simply standing and having a heated conversation and debate with each other. They were trying to be children: smiling, chasing one another, with no stress or worry, but instead full of joy.

The school bell rang; it was time to start class. Every child was running into his or her own classroom. Some children, who came from far away, could be seen running across the fields to class. Others, who were late, tried to sneak through gaps in the fence, and from there, into the classroom, hoping to avoid being caught.

Marama was a science teacher. He loved teaching. He remembered how his parents would speak positively about teachers: they were like parents, they would say, and should be respected. In the school where Marama was placed, the children had great need of stable, kind authority: they needed their teachers to be like parents. They had already experienced significant hardship.

In the mid-1980s in Ethiopia, amid drought and famine, approximately half a million people died of hunger. Some 5.8 million people became dependent on relief. The regime's response was to uproot some 600 000 people in the affected areas and resettle them in the south. Many were moved forcibly; families were split, and many died on the journey, as well as at the destination, where little or no preparations had been made to receive these arrivals. Many of them ended up in Asosa, at Marama's school. When he talks about the children whose lives he tried to save, he has to stop to weep.

They were all just starting a new life

Before class started, I took the daily roster, as I did every day. I was marking the names of the children, both present and absent. It was my second year of teaching at the school – 1989. It is called *Komeshiga Primary* or elementary school with children aged between eight and 16, approximately. A few of the children were locals, but most came from the north of the country, and had been resettled in Asosa. Thousands of people were displaced in the country at that time. They were all just starting a new life. These were nail-biting situations, and it was a challenge for them to keep going.

By the time Marama took up his first teaching post in 1985, the country was in the grip of a brutal civil war. Ethiopia was ruled by the Derg, a group of Marxist army officers, who had seized power in a military coup. Their chairman was Mengistu Haile Mariam. Political opposition to Mengistu's brutal regime was largely expressed in ethnic terms. Different minorities mobilised and formed rebel groups. This was yet another of the many proxy wars fought in the name of the Cold War. The Derg, armed by the Soviet Union, found itself ranged against the Eritrean People's Liberation Front (EPLF) fighting for Eritrean independence, the Tigrayan People's Front, and, later, the Oromo Liberation Front.

Then the nightmare started

Everyone felt fearful that week. It was easy to see the anxiety of the people living in the area. No one knew what was going on. There was a rumour of war in the area. The army battalion observable in the area belonged to the government. They could be seen patrolling the area. Sometimes they caught and beat people, if they suspected them of transferring information to the opposition forces fighting in the bush.

After I took the roll, I turned to the writing board at the front of the class, in the middle of the hall, to write the class activities for the day. The first sound I heard was the huge explosion that left us all extremely terrified. The first explosion hit the schoolyard. It dusted the soil on the roof of the building. Within less than a minute the second explosion repeated but hit outside of the school ground, a few metres from the building. Then the nightmare started. The shooting was everywhere. Bombs were dropping on every corner of the building and in the area. Bullets were raining from every angle. From the loud bangs of heavy ammunition to the sounds of small bullets, noise was echoing all over the ground and in the bush. We could hear fire-spitting ammunition coming from the direction of the mountains.

Marama's school was situated in an area that was convenient for military strategy. The school sat in a valley, and on the hilltops on either side, rebels faced off against government forces. In a major offensive, the Eritrean People's Liberation Front, together with the Oromo Liberation Front, were fighting the Derg.

I am not sure how many died

The schoolchildren were running in all directions. They were trying to jump over the fence, or to roll under it. They were falling on the ground everywhere, trampling each other in a rush. It was complete chaos that morning. It looked like a nightmare. Everywhere could be heard the screaming of children. More than one hundred of them were able to run into the surrounding bush. I assume that many were injured. I am not sure how many of them died.

We were surrounded by dense bushland that started a few hundred metres from the school building. The bushy hills began at the schoolyard, and ran for hundreds of kilometres until they connected with the other mountain ranges. There was no village, no farm, no ordinary people doing ordinary activities. There were only armed soldiers. Anyone who ran about 100 metres from the schoolground could easily join the bush and disappear. It was not easy to find a person if they were hiding in the area. It could take days. If people wanted, they could follow the mountains and travel until they reached the border without coming across villages. But most of the time it was rare to escape attack, either from wild animals or 'human animals'.

Most of us ran to the bush. We ran as far into the forest as we could. The bushes and trees were very dense. It was not easy to run as fast as we wanted to. The good thing was the dense bush gave us protection because we could hide. We were about 20 teachers. On that day we were not able to get far away from the area. Everyone felt frustrated. The sounds of shooting and ammunition explosion were everywhere in the field, and in the mountains. A helicopter was coming and dropping explosives at regular intervals. We heard the blast in the sky. We observed the smoke of a fire that probably came from the bombs falling on surrounding villages and farms.

When I asked Marama why they did not wait in the bush, and return once the fighting had ended, he explained to me that the fighting had been going on for years. That in Derg-run Ethiopia, there was just one government-controlled radio station, and any other news was rumour. So all that they knew was that there was war. The children he taught had already been displaced: the 'home' they ran from was a temporary one. These were people conditioned by long years of war, by attacks on civilians, not to feel safe. These experiences, and the lack of any reliable news, meant that they did not know where they could safely seek refuge in Ethiopia. So instead, they left the school, and their lives, behind, and began what was to be an arduous, two-week-long journey.

Whatever they let us keep to wear

We stayed the night on the mountain. In the early morning, we started pushing forward on the footpath in the bush. In my group, we were about 200 people. We all followed one another, staying in a line in the forest under the bottom of the mountain. Those able to walk fast were leading, while others looked exhausted, hardly taking steps in the hills of the mountains. Everyone walked in groups. People who had fled the village like us were with us in that long, tiring trip. No one knew each other but the disaster of the war collected us all together in the mountains.

On the second day, after we travelled about five hours, we saw one small village from a distance. It looked empty. We selected about ten people from our group and sent them to the village, to get us food if possible. The food did not have to be cooked. Even uncooked grains would be fine, just to put something in our mouth and to survive, not to die.

They did not take long, and within one hour they came back to us with about 100 kilograms of uncooked corn. We shared the corn as much as we could. Everyone got a fair share although not enough. We had no issues with drinking water. Every hole contained water that accumulated from the rain in the winter. Floods from the mountains formed small lakes and waterfalls. Every lowland was full of water. We just had to push aside dried leaves and grasses and drink it.

On the second day, we continued our journey by following the low hills that stretched among huge mountains. Our aim was to travel until we reached somewhere or saw villages. No one was familiar with the area. But we still felt that we had not travelled far enough away from the region where the battle was taking place. After we travelled for about half a day, we reached the big river in the area called Dabus River. Local people who assisted others to cross lived on the river's edge. To get across the river, we were asked to pay, roughly about 25 cents. However, it was a lot of money in this part of Ethiopia. It was not easy to get such an amount of money. It was an excellent business opportunity for the owner of the boat.

We, the teachers, contributed whatever coins and notes we had in our pockets. We gathered a reasonable amount that convinced the people to help us cross the river. We begged them to pass the children for free. Many of us stood in the middle of the river to ferry the children across. Very few of us were able to swim. Even for those able to swim it was a dangerous river. First, the river flowed down from between two high mountains at high pressure. Second, they told us it is not safe to swim as we would probably be attacked by sharks.

After we all crossed the river, we asked if someone was available to guide us to the border of the country. We told them we needed someone trusted who knew the route and who could keep us safely hidden as much as possible if our journey became risky. They told us it would cost a considerable amount of money. We had no other alternatives.

We begged a lot again through local elders, and they finally agreed to find us people from the area with some of the money that we still had after the river crossing. After hours of searching, they found us a couple of people. They looked young, in their twenties. But they seemed very confident with the journey and the route, and they had had many experiences travelling to the border of the country for trade and other business in the past. For sure, the first day they were very comfortable and supportive. After we travelled a lot, crossing many hills, mountains, rivers and deserts we stopped in one of the open spaces between mountains to sleep the night there. Now, after we had travelled for a whole day, we started to sense that we were close to remote areas.

Once we had settled down to sleep the night, the guides told us that they would not continue guiding us the next day. They told us that they were frightened of travelling in the region with so many people. They told us the small amount of money we paid was not enough for the high risk they were taking. They simply left in the night without telling us they were returning and without even giving us any indication of what we could do.

Without a plan, and with no control over our situation, we stayed in the same place in the hills for about four days. We allocated ourselves into groups, and took turns travelling in the area to find any sort of food. Everyone took precautions when wandering in the area to search for food. We knew the local people would not attack us. But we were very scared, in case armed groups came into the area. There was no food or anything to eat. By searching on foot, one of the groups found a small village in the area. The village was more than three hours' walk from the place where we were hiding. We went to the village and begged for any food they could give us, especially for the children. Luckily they helped us a lot with what they had. They boiled grains and gave this to us. Sometimes, just to survive, we had to look for tree fruits, roots and leaves to eat.

On our fifth day, we found three new people who could lead us through the bare bush to the border. The local elders supported us a lot. They found us the escape route guides. We gave them whatever we had left. Many of the teachers handed them their watches and rings. Some of us gave them jackets, and we left with shirts, singlets and pants, whatever they let us keep to wear.

We travelled in the night for many hours and slept in the hills during the daytime. We continued for three nights. It was very exhausting. Travelling in the desert was not easy. On top of all that, we were scared about what would wait for us on the border.

Our guides told us to stay in one of the hills, while they went to assess the area before we continued on the journey. We accepted their command. We trusted them. After a few hours they came back and told us not to move today, that it would be safer to continue our journey the following morning. They told us that we were very close to the border. Luckily, it was a semi-desert area. There was no human activity in the area. It was open and clear with a straight path that showed our footsteps clearly, so that we could follow each other in the sand. We could easily see the direction we were heading in, from a distance.

Our guides told us to follow the footpath and continue travelling until we saw one of the camps. They also told us that it would take a whole day of walking, or half a day if we were able to walk quickly. They wished us good luck with it, and the three of them left us there and returned home.

Marama, together with the surviving children and teachers, came, via the town of Kurmuk on the Ethiopian–Sudanese border, to the refugee camp in Yabus. Here, the 12 teachers that remained acted as both teachers and parents to the 120 children in their care. Eight teachers and more than 80 children had been lost on the long march; some had broken off from the group to try a different path. Others had been killed in the initial attack. Marama tells me that he would be surprised if anyone who did not flee had survived the fighting. Marama quotes an African proverb: 'When elephants fight, it is the grass that suffers.' But even flight was no guarantee of survival.

I was starting refugee life

If the journey had been safe and straightforward, it would not have taken us more than a week to reach the border. But we had to travel slowly. There were many times when our guides went ahead to assess the area and then came back to tell us to keep moving forward. On top of all that, it was autumn, and the weather was hot. It was very hard to walk in the middle of the day for the adults, let alone the children.

We started walking early in the morning on that day. We kept travelling for almost half a day. Then suddenly we approached a small camp. We saw a few people moving around the field wearing some uniforms. When we were close to them, we were asked to stop where we were. It was a commanding voice, sharp and strong. Most of us were already used to such voices, from our country, and our region. The loud call was similar. It was a military voice giving the order. We already recognised them as they were armies of the neighbouring country. We all were terrified. We did not know them; they did not know us. They told us to walk to one of the open fields in a queue. We did so. They provided us with water and food to eat from their store. They already identified us as refugees fleeing war in the neighbouring country. I guess they had already been exposed to similar experiences in the past as many refugees like us crossed the border in similar footsteps and surrendered themselves to armies.

After we had eaten, they brought big trucks to take us to another side of the border. Because of the uneven, hilly road, the truck took about six hours to reach a small camp in the desert. We arrived at the camp and realised that it was arranged to accommodate new refugees. There were small huts made of bamboo trees. We were allocated our shelters as a group of people. The camp was made up of mostly empty huts, with just a few armed soldiers patrolling. From that day I convinced myself that I had at least been saved from death and was starting refugee life.

When you suddenly run from death

If the people guiding us left us in the middle of the mountains, in the middle of nowhere, what would have happened to us? If they handed us to other smugglers what would have happened to us? Not one of us made themselves ready for such an unexpected disaster. When you suddenly run from death it is not easy to make yourself ready for unforeseen circumstances. We had nothing in our hands, and we were helpless and hopeless before even the minor obstacles we encountered during that time.

After travelling for about two weeks in danger, we finally arrived at the destination we never expected. It was a refugee camp that had just been established. There were a few empty huts. Unfortunately, the field was on the crossing of two main roads. If an armed clash took place in the area, it would be a strategic place. The camp was thousands of miles away from towns in a remote area. It was very common to observe dangerous wild animals wandering around in mobs.

In the camp in Yabus, Marama was reunited with one of his sisters, who had found her way there, together with her three children. Marama met his wife in the camp, and they spent nine and a half years there. It was a dangerous place. His sister and her eldest child did not survive their time in Yabus. Her surviving son eventually made his life in Canada. Her daughter came with Marama and his wife to Australia, when they were granted refugee status. Two of the schoolchildren also came to Australia.

'Refugee'

Refugee ... A human being who is neglected while still breathing and alive. A human being cut off from everything. A human being who is detested while still thriving.

Refugee ... A human being criminalised for a cause never known to them. Running away from the danger that came to them by a body unknown to them, running away to safety from danger.

Refugee ... Telling them to make a queue and counting them all the time, selecting among them, those who can travel and leave, those who seem like a burden on the way, as they travel through the desert with smugglers.

Refugee ... A human being who becomes a commodity, and who is used to generate income through smuggling.

Refugee ... A victim but victimless. Blamed but blameless. Story unfolds.

While he was in the camp in Yabus, Marama chose not to return to Ethiopia. Initially, this was because return would not be safe. Since Marama came to Australia, Ethiopia has twice been at war: with Eritrea, from 1998 to 2000, and Somalia, from 2006 to 2008. As years went on, Ethiopia became an increasingly distant place for Marama; a place that was no longer home, and where reintegration would mean starting again. Now, Ethiopia carries the trauma of Marama's journey: putting his life, and those of the children for whom he felt responsible in the hands of smugglers. Marama now lives in an outer suburb of Melbourne, where he works to help other refugees overcome their own trauma, and make a new life in Australia.

A passionate advocate for peace

I came to Australia as a refugee on a humanitarian visa for resettlement with my wife and niece at the end of 1999. I am a passionate activist for peace, stability and human rights. After I arrived in Australia, I gained additional professional qualifications through study that gave me the opportunity to work towards being an advocate for sustainable community development. I am extensively involved in anti-conflict, anti-war, and peace and stability campaigns, advocacy and lobbying activities through the Horn of African communities; in particular, the Oromo and Ethiopian communities in Australia.

9

MUNJED AL MUDERIS:
A JOURNEY OF MANY LEGS

with Ruth Balint

Munjed comes from one of Iraq's nine traditional ruling families, and his grandfather was once the head of the Sunni faith in large parts of Iraq and the Muslim world. But in 1980, when Munjed was seven years old, the Iran–Iraq War broke out, which lasted for eight years, devastating Iraq's economy. The rise of Saddam Hussein to power, and Iraq's invasion of Kuwait, which led to the First Gulf War in 1990, wreaked further social and economic havoc. Munjed had originally planned to go to medical school in New York. Instead he went first to Basra, a city on the border to Kuwait, then to Anbar University, and eventually to Baghdad University Hospital, where he was able to finish his university studies.

In the late 1990s, when Munjed graduated, Iraq was at war with the United States and Iraqis were living under the brutal dictatorship of Saddam Hussein. Inflation had soared and the economy had collapsed. After his one-year internship as a medical graduate, Munjed was accepted into the surgical training program. This was a dream come true. But soon afterwards, as he began his rounds one November morning in the 1200-bed general hospital in Baghdad, three buses full of army deserters arrived under control of the military police. The medical staff were ordered to abandon all planned surgery and operate on the army deserters, disfiguring them by removing the tops of their ears. Munjed described what happened next in his book Walking Free:

I saw three burly officers striding along the corridor towards the operating theatre. They were menacingly huge, heavily armed and dressed in full camouflage uniform with combat boots – the most finely honed instruments of Saddam's brutality. As they approached they were giving orders to staff to immediately begin the surgery. The most senior doctor in the operating theatre refused their instructions. He told the officers he had taken a solemn oath to do no harm to his patients. Straight away he was marched to the hospital carpark, briefly interrogated and then shot in front of a number of medical staff. The military thugs then came back to the operating theatre and bluntly told us: 'If anyone shares his view, step forward. Otherwise carry on.'

I was confronted by the greatest dilemma of my life.[1]

Munjed hid in the women's toilets for five hours, after which he fled. He went straight to a friend of his, who drove him to Ramadi, a city in Anbar province, where he had once spent a year of his studies. He stayed with a contact for three days. During an afternoon in Sydney, he discussed his first encounter with people smugglers, who he described as people working 'in the system'.

That was my first encounter with people smugglers

While I was hiding out in Ramadi, my friend and I met with two men. One was in police uniform, the other one was in normal civilian clothes. They were both senior Passport Office police. I gave them money, and enlisted the help of my cousin in Baghdad, an army intelligence officer, to get photos to them to prepare a fake passport for me. These two men prepared the fake passport after a couple of days, which they handed to me after I gave them another large sum of money. Now I was no longer a doctor but a handyman. Doctors weren't allowed to leave the country at this time. I signed the new passport, and added my thumbprint using the ink pad the two officers had brought with them. They also agreed to remove my name from the computer list of people who were forbidden to leave the country, at one border checkpoint into Jordan, for just two hours. I had to be at the crossing at Trebil the next afternoon when my name would temporarily disappear from the list. So that was my first encounter with people smugglers. I don't know how I look at these people or how I (should) classify them, but these people saved my life in one way.

Munjed managed to get through the border checkpoint at Trebil with his fake passport, and travelled into Jordan, eventually arriving in Amman. His first impression was of the hundreds of Iraqi men, standing around smoking and talking. They would have been working as low-paid labourers as they waited either for their refugee applications to be accepted by the United Nations High Commissioner for Refugees (UNHCR), or for people smugglers to take them to Europe. Amman was known as a hotspot for people smuggling at this time.

I didn't have any idea where I was going

Jordan was not safe because it was controlled by the Iraqi intelligence services. I decided very quickly I couldn't stay there. Malaysia was one country where it was possible, as an Iraqi national, to live and work. You had to get a 14-day visa, and then extend it for three months by enrolling in an educational course. So I decided to go there, and bought my ticket for a flight on Gulf Air.

We landed in Abu Dhabi. We were in transit for about three hours. All the Iraqi nationals had their passports confiscated by the immigration officers in transit, because they didn't want the Iraqis slipping out of the airport and into Abu Dhabi. I was sitting near two young men, who looked very rough, they were like handymen and they couldn't speak a word of English. They were anxious about getting their passports back. In Abu Dhabi nobody speaks Arabic, though ironically it's an Arabic country, and I told them I would interpret for them and that they would get their documents back when we boarded the plane again. Then I asked them a question: 'Where are you guys going?' They looked at me and they said, 'Oh, we are tourists.' And I said, 'Yeah right. You don't look touristy to me. You don't speak a word of English, and you don't know what you're doing.' So they said to me, 'OK, we'll take you with us if you help us with interpreting.' And I said, 'Yeah that's a good idea.' I didn't have any idea where I was going. I just had to leave.

We landed in Kuala Lumpur. I helped them to fill in their immigration forms which were in English and then we went to the immigration checkpoint. Funnily enough, for one of them, his passport was going to expire which meant he wouldn't be allowed into Malaysia. I intervened and promised the customs officer that he would go to the Iraqi Embassy straight away once he left the airport and renew the passport. I persuaded the officer to let him through. So anyway, once we were through the immigration process, they had to find a public phone box. They had a phone number. We found a phone and dialled the number. This guy on the line, he said, 'Come and meet me in Chow Kit.' Chow Kit is a busy area, also known as a red-light district, full of massage parlours and traders selling fake Louis Vuitton bags and watches.

Munjed and the two Iraqis took a taxi to meet their contact. As Munjed has described it, he suddenly found himself in the middle of a people-smuggling operation.

I'm a respectable smuggler!

When we got out of the taxi he was standing in front of McDonald's. He was wearing a hat and a brown shirt, brown shorts. And he looked like Steve Irwin basically, he was blond, tanned, with blue eyes. And I started talking to him in English and he was, you know, surprised that I was speaking English. He turned out to be an Iraqi Kurd, who had lived in Kuala Lumpur for a long time. His name was Mahdi. He took us to a small hotel up the road, and told us, 'Give me this sum of money', which was very significant, 'and give me your passports and I'll get back to you with your next destination tomorrow.'

I mean I was astonished at how competent this guy was. But I said, 'Well, hang on. How do you expect me to trust you with my passport and this amount of money, and that you will come back tomorrow?' And he got really offended. And he said, 'How dare you question my credibility. I'm a respectable smuggler. I have a job to protect and a reputation to protect.' And he was very genuine with the way he spoke and he said, 'Do you think we play games here? We are in serious business.'

I mean, it was a very tough night for me, I didn't sleep. I didn't have my passport on me, and I had paid him a large amount of money. I mean money was not an issue for me, it was the passport itself. I would be stuck in Malaysia. If I went to the Iraqi Embassy or the UNHCR or anywhere, I would be arrested, put back in a plane back to Iraq and executed. So it was a very difficult situation. I didn't have a choice. But he turned out to be a respectable smuggler.

Most people, like Munjed, who begin their journeys in the Middle East come via Southeast Asia: Munjed followed a common route through Malaysia, which does not require visas for travellers from many Middle Eastern countries for short stays. Indonesia is the most common transit country for making the last leg of the journey to Australia by boat. It is also cheaper to survive there for long periods compared with Malaysia.

A man of his word

He came back the next day. And he had brought us first-class tickets with Garuda Airlines to Jakarta, with a visa stamped in our passports. His job was to get us to Indonesia, beyond that he didn't want to be involved, even though I asked him where we were headed after that. But he was not just, you know, a man of his word, if that makes any sense. He was also very accurate and precise. 'When you land in Jakarta,' he said, 'you will land at this time of the night, in the early hours of the morning, and you will see a number of customs officers in front of you. Do not go to the covered woman, do not go to the guy with the beard, do not go to the guy with too many stars. Go to the guy with one star, put one hundred dollars inside your passport and give him your passport and he will let you in.'

And I looked at him. 'Hang on,' I said. 'You expect me to bribe a customs officer in a major international airport?' I mean, this was really way off the acceptable range of bribery! And he said, 'Yeah. Do you have a problem with that?'

'Obviously, you know, it's wrong on so many levels.' But it was exactly as he described it. He was so accurate and everything went very smoothly. And it's funny that one of the two guys (I was travelling with), got a bit greedy and he put 50 dollars inside his passport, not 100, and the customs officer wouldn't let him in. Yeah. And it was a glitch that we had to rectify very quickly.

Munjed and the two Iraqis dialled a number they had been given for Omeed the people smuggler, who told them the name of a hotel on the outskirts of Jakarta.

I'm Omeed the smuggler

The hotel was a six-storey building that was really rundown. And (there were) hundreds and hundreds of Middle Eastern–looking people with Middle Eastern clothes, and covered Muslim women. It was a very depressing and dire picture. We sat in the foyer and we started talking to people and the stories that we heard were that people had been stuck there for months and months. A lot of them had lost all their money and they were desperate, they didn't know where they were going, what was happening to them.

At that moment these two guys who had accompanied me or whom I had accompanied, saved my life. Basically they started telling people, 'This guy is a doctor!' That was the first time I realised that doctors can be of use in the smuggling industry. So I mean, it's very funny that I went to my room very depressed and I thought that this is it. I'm gonna be stuck here for God knows. And then, a couple of hours later, there was a knock on my door and this time there was this guy wearing black, he had a black beard, black hair. I opened the door and he said, 'Oh, are you the doctor?'

'Yes, I am the doctor.'

'Well, I prayed to God that God would provide me with a doctor.'

'OK, what can I do for you?'

'I'm Omeed the smuggler.'

He was speaking with broken Arabic and pretending to be an Arab Shi'ite. But he was a Sunni Kurd.

'I have a brand-new boat that's going to Australia in three days and I need a doctor on the boat.'

'What's the reason?'

'I have this *mullah*, *iman*, who is bringing with him a piece of clay that's mixed with Muhammad the prophet's grandson's blood and it's holy clay. So he will sprinkle dust from that clay to calm the waters, calm the sea, so the boat can have a safe journey.'

'Wow, that's really brilliant technology. Everybody should have that.'

'But I have a problem: the *mullah* has a daughter who is heavily pregnant and I need a doctor to look after the daughter and the other people on the boat, so they can reach their destination safely. I make sure that there is a doctor on every boat that goes.'

So I'm wondering whether this guy has some sense of responsibility. And then he asked me, 'What do you need?' And I said, 'Well, how many people are there on the boat?' And he said, 'Around fifty and it's brand new.'

'I need one hundred drips, one hundred giving sets, like saline bags. A lot of cannulas and a lot of injections for nausea, and tablets for seasickness.'

'OK I'll get you all of that.'

'How can you get me all of that, these are medical supplies! You can't just go and buy them from the chemist.'

'Don't you worry, I have a lot of connections.'

I mean he seemed to know what he was doing and the next day he brought all the medical supplies exactly as I had described them and he said, 'Is that what you want?' I said, 'Yeah, that's brilliant.' And then we went and got a lot of baguettes, a lot of canned tuna and other canned food and a lot of bottles of water and Coke.

A significant number of refugees who board boats to Australia have already been found to be refugees by the UNHCR, but have waited years to get to Australia legally. Indonesia is not a signatory to the United Nations 1951 Refugee Convention, but certified refugees can remain in Indonesia as they await resettlement in a third country. They cannot legally work, access public services or obtain citizenship. Some are held in this homeless limbo for years. Munjed paid Omeed $2000 for the boat trip, but the usual fee was a lot higher.

They stripped people of their belongings

A day or two later the journey started in the early hours of the morning. We were 50 people on a bus. The bus journey took hours and hours and then we got to the southern port of Java, to an abandoned village. Omeed was there, but he was accompanied by an Indonesian guy in a brand-new Mercedes-Benz, and there were also two armed security guards. They had big machine guns. Before long, two other buses arrived and we ended up being 165 people, not 50! They started stripping people of their belongings, everything, watches, jewellery, whatever money they had left, in order to get on the boat.

The refugees were ferried to a boat in the harbour aboard a small tinnie, a handful at a time. It was night-time. The whole operation took four hours.

We were crammed like sardines

The sun started rising and then we started the journey. I noticed that the smuggler Omeed had sent his younger brother with us on the boat. He told a few people and asked them to keep it secret so the Australian police did not capture him and interrogate him. He died eventually in a car crash in Perth.

We were crammed like sardines in a leaky boat, a tiny fishing boat. And it had one hold-all in the middle, in the bottom, to store fish. People were crammed in there. Obviously a lot of these people who came from the Middle East had never seen the sea before. They thought this was the safest place. But this hole had no ventilation. A lot of them became comatose and nearly suffocated. So we tried to bring them up.

People started vomiting as soon as we reached the open seas. Then they lost control of their bladders. And the boat was leaking. People were carrying buckets of water. You know, this was a leaky wooden boat like a fishing boat with one diesel engine, six-cylinder, a truck engine and so it was hopeless. There were no life rafts, no emergency beacons, only a few life jackets. It was horrible.

After a few hours, I saw that there was a big grey ship with white numbers written on it, tailing us. A small black dinghy from that ship came alongside us. We had this Indonesian fishing captain with us and he looked at us and with broken English pointed and said, 'Straight Christmas Island. Miss, two weeks, mainland.'

That was all the navigation advice that we got. And then he jumped on to that dinghy and went back to the main ship. It was a military ship. And we were left to face the elements on our own. Lucky we had an Iraqi sailor who had escaped from the Iraqi navy with us on the boat and he could read charts, and he took over the boat.

Munjed has described how the journey proceeded from that point. 'The ill-fated boat was battling the elements, its little engine, built for nothing more boisterous than the waters directly off the Indonesian coast, chugging and complaining in a constant battle with the increasingly angry ocean waves crashing against the hull. The accompanying soundtrack was the chilling noise of people moaning and throwing up.' Added to this was heavy rain that suddenly came down, continuing that way for hours, and then the wind that turned the sea into a roller coaster. On board, the refugees were weakening from dehydration and illness, among them three heavily pregnant women.

It was horrible

I was so busy that I didn't get a chance to get seasick. I had to constantly put in drips and IV lines, including for the *mullah's* daughter. She was sitting in the area where they kept the women and she was fully covered from top to bottom and she started vomiting. She was heavily pregnant and I wanted to put a drip in her to give a fluid and she put her arm up for me fully clothed and I said, 'Yeah right. What do you want me to do with this?' And she said, 'Put the drip.' And I said, 'Where? Through the clothes?'

I mean, I can't tolerate this kind of stupidity. And then her father, the *mullah* came. 'He's a doctor', he told her. 'He's allowed to see your arm.' You know, the boat was rocking and I mean it was terrible. I said, 'Look I don't have time for this shit. Obviously your father's clay didn't work. Maybe made in China.'

By the time we got to Christmas Island there were less than ten of us that had stayed vertical out of 165 and the rest were lying on top of each other on the floor. It was horrible. It was absolutely putrefying. We got to Christmas Island on 8 November 1999. The Australian Federal Police intercepted us about a mile from the shore. We told them we were asylum seekers.

From Christmas Island Munjed was sent to Curtin Detention Centre for nine months, an experience he has described as hell on earth.

I had no other choice

If you ask me the question would I do it again, I would say you bet I would because I had no other choice. I didn't have any other options. All the countries that I went through, they were not signatories to the Refugee Convention of 1951. So I had no place to go.

I was released from the detention centre on 26 August 2000 and I started working immediately and I worked as a toilet cleaner to start with and then I applied for jobs as a doctor. I received my first paycheque on 1 November 2000 so I wasted taxpayers' money for two months living on a Centrelink social security card. I'm not dissimilar to many people who were brought up knowing that work is an honour, the person who is capable of working and chooses not to is a person that doesn't have any honour.

Munjed first found work as a doctor in the Emergency Unit in Mildura Hospital. He went on to work in various hospitals, and at the same time, sat and passed the Royal Australasian College of Surgeons exams as a general surgeon. He was finally admitted to the four-year Australian Orthopaedic Association's training program in 2005. He sat the final exam of his training program in 2008, while he was based at Westmead Hospital, and passed it first time.

We have to have acceptance

Every time I stand and give a talk, I say, well, you know, hang on guys, 70 years ago or 80 years ago people were killed based on their identity, massive genocide happened, and now we're forgetting and we're returning back to saying the same things that were said in the '30s. It's about discrimination against race, ethnic background or religion. And that is wrong. And the thing is now it's about the Muslims. And a hundred years ago it was the Chinese. There's always someone getting labelled the outsider who needs to be exterminated. And we cannot allow that. I mean the world cannot tolerate this kind of behaviour, it should never tolerate this kind of behaviour. This kind of attitude should be eradicated, like eradicating polio or leprosy, because it is a disease.

You know, we have to have tolerance. We have to have acceptance of each other and we cannot name people based on their colour or race. You know people should be accountable for what they do, not the way they look or their heritage or their beliefs. I have people coming to me constantly, refugees, and the system is set up to destroy them and not give them a chance to become successful. And I spend a lot of time trying to encourage them to rise above it and to think smart about how they will act.

Munjed has since become Australia's most celebrated refugee. He is an orthopaedic surgeon and a clinical professor at Macquarie University and the Australian School of Advanced Medicine. He specialises in hip, knee, trauma and osseointegration surgery. He is a fellow of the Royal Australasian College of Surgeons and Chairman of the Osseointegration Group of Australia. His work as an osseointegration surgeon, which means fitting amputees with robotic legs, is recognised as revolutionary and world leading. His position and his reputation as a pioneering medical surgeon have also given him a unique platform to speak out against Australia's refugee detention regime, which he himself endured as a boat person from Iraq in 2000. He is a passionate advocate for human rights. In 2020, he became the NSW Australian of the Year.

10

TAOZEN: ENTREPRENEUR

with Julie Kalman

Taozen cuts a striking figure when we meet on a September morning. A tall man, he wears a colourful cap and scarf that I later learn identifies him as Hazara. He lives in the outer suburbs of Melbourne and leads a very busy life. Since arriving in Melbourne in 2000, Taozen has gained qualifications as a driving instructor, a mortgage broker and a real estate agent. He has achieved diplomas in community development and business management. He volunteered with the Country Fire Authority. In 2014, Taozen ran as a candidate for The Greens in the Victorian parliamentary elections, and he remains involved in state politics. As we go to press, Taozen has completed a Masters of Entrepreneurship and Innovation, and he intends to keep studying. But Taozen works hard, too, in refugee advocacy. His response when I contacted him to ask if we could meet was generous. Over a series of conversations, Taozen told me his story. We met, each time, in outer Melbourne, where Taozen is very much at home. He took me to a café run by Hazaras, where we were served strong tea, along with the sweets that melt in your mouth as you drink.

The violence that marked Taozen's childhood

Taozen was born in the city of Ghazni in 1978, in the province of the same name. Both are strategically important. The city is situated 150 kilometres from Afghanistan's capital, Kabul, and lies between Kabul and the country's second-largest city, Kandahar. Taozen's earliest years were punctuated by the events that set the lives of Afghanis on a downward spiral. There aren't many countries, as Amin Saikal has written in his history of Afghanistan, that have 'sustained as many blows, and such hard blows, as has Afghanistan'.[1] Afghanistan's recent story is one of a state where political and societal structures are weak. Successive rulers and governments practised personal, rather than institutional politics, and this led to national disunity, socio-economic instability, and the complete lack of any legitimacy and transparency in government, placing Afghanistan at the mercy of radicalism from within, and of power rivalries from without.

When Taozen was just one year old, the People's Democratic Party of Afghanistan (PDPA) seized power from the ruling royal family in a military coup. President Daoud was executed, along with 18 members of his family, including his wife, his children and his grandchildren. They were buried in unmarked graves. That afternoon, Afghanistan's new rulers announced the coup over national radio. The military who had taken power quickly established a civilian government. It allied with the Soviet Union, and embarked on radical reforms, including the cancellation of debts for landless farmers, a move that was highly unpopular. The regime repressed any resistance with great brutality. But resistance to the regime and its ambitions was strong, particularly by mujahedin, or Islamist groups. Islam became the ideology of resistance, supported by the United States against the Soviet-backed Communist regime, in yet another of the many proxy wars that punctuated the Cold War. In December 1979, seeking to stabilise and thus save the regime, Soviet forces invaded. Afghanistan was to have the distinction of hosting the Cold War's final battle. Thirty thousand Soviet troops were deployed to prop up the state, against US support for the mujahedin rebellion. Soon after invasion, the original Soviet forces were bolstered by the arrival of tens of thousands more troops, making more than 100 000 Soviet troops in the country. The Soviets controlled the cities and large towns, while the mujahedin had relative freedom in the countryside. Soviet troops fought to crush the rebels, using air power to destroy villages and thus deny safe haven to the rebels, and laying millions of land mines. The rebels, who employed guerrilla tactics to elude attacks, maintained fierce resistance. The Afghan Civil War raged for over 14 years. Ordinary Afghans fled: by 1982, hundreds of thousands of people had made their way to Pakistan and to Iran.

This was the violence that marked Taozen's childhood. The main activity in Ghazni is farming, which is what Taozen's parents did, in a remote farming village, called Jaghuri.

We are a tiny farming village, of a couple of hundred houses, and a few shops, but mainly people survive on cultivating the land manually. I was helping [my parents] on the farm. I probably had a tiny amount of sheep and cattle, I would take them to pasture and then sometimes our neighbour would say, 'Can you take mine as well?' I said, 'That's fine.' They give me bread and a good meal, I was happy to take them along as well.

Taozen was the second son; two more boys and two girls were soon added to his family. There was long-standing institutional prejudice against Hazaras in Afghanistan, and Hazaristan was deliberately kept undeveloped and poor. When Taozen was growing up, there were just a few local schools, and education was very basic. Children were taught to read the holy texts, and to write. Taozen's father was an Islamic scholar, an expert on the Koran and other Arabic texts. Taozen studied with him at home. He learned to read using the holy texts, and through the works of Khwāja Shams-ud-din Muhammad Hafiz, a Sufi poet, whose writings are considered some of the very best, and most beautiful, ever to be written.

When the trouble started

The fact of being Hazara is central to Taozen's story. In one sense, Taozen has had no choice but to embrace his ethnicity: the physical appearance of the Hazara people makes them stand out in Afghanistan. Hazaras look like the people of Central Asia, and this has set them apart from the majority Pashtun Afghanis, among whom Hazaras have lived for centuries. This difference is one reason for their persecution, which has led to their exile across the globe, with large communities in Pakistan, Iran, the Gulf States, Australia, the United States and Europe. Another reason is the fact that they are mostly Shia Muslims, in a country where some 80 per cent of the population follows Sunni Islam.

No one is certain when the Hazaras first settled in Afghanistan, but it is thought that they came with Genghis Khan's Mongol soldiers when they swept through the region, some 800 years ago. Today, they are the third-largest group, after the majority Pashtuns and the Tajiks, in a country shared by fourteen recognised ethnic groups. They are more or less equal in number with Uzbeks, forming somewhere between 9 and 20 per cent of the broader population. They speak Hazaragi, a Persian dialect very close to Dari, one of the two official languages of the country (the other is Pashto). Historically, Hazaras have lived in the mountainous centre of the country, across a number of different provinces, in a region generally called Hazarajat. This region is under-developed, and the bulk of the population survives by farming. Today, they also live across much of Afghanistan, including in the capital, Kabul, where they make up a large minority.

Ghazni region, where Taozen was born, is ethnically diverse, a gathering place for many of the different peoples who inhabit Afghanistan. Hazaras make – or, rather, made – up the largest of these groups, including Tajiks and Pashtuns. This is where he spent his childhood. When Taozen tells me about Ghazni, he takes care to stress that he prefers his region to be called Hazaristan. The 'jat' in Hazarajat, he tells me, is diminutive, pejorative. It implies a scattering of people, rather than a well-defined people. The suffix 'stan', on the other hand, is used for nations, and implies a homeland: a place where one stays. If the Tajiks and Uzbeks have their 'stan', he asks me, then why not the Hazaras?

What might seem like a quibble over a simple suffix is anything but petty. Behind Taozen's preference is a century and more of brutal persecution. For most of the twentieth century, Hazaras have faced considerable political, social and economic disadvantage. Hazaras worked in low-paying jobs in the cities and towns of Afghanistan, or they stayed in Hazaristan, eking out a living from farming. Members of the lower classes made their way to the cities of Afghanistan, looking for work. The writer Khaled Hosseini sought to bring this disadvantage to light with his creation of the Hazara characters Ali and Hassan in The Kite Runner.

Under Soviet rule, Hazaras did not fare any worse than other groups. Religion, of course, became suspect, and religious leaders would disappear. But Hazaras formed resistance groups, based in Iran. In this way, they rebuilt leadership, and emerged as an independent, self-confident force. In February 1989, Soviet troops left Afghanistan after a failed occupation. By the time the Soviets pulled out, Hazaras were ready to lay claim to the rights they had been denied for so long. But things were to become much, much worse. In 1992, the government collapsed, and three years later, in 1995, the Taliban took over. Taozen was 17.

The Taliban were Pashtun, Sunni Muslims and deeply fundamentalist. They declared war on the Hazara. In the mid-1990s, speaking to a crowd in northern Afghanistan, Taliban commander Maulawi Mohammed Hanif is reported to have told a crowd: 'Hazaras are not Muslims, you can kill them.' In January 1995, the Taliban took control of Ghazni. They were looking for weapons and for young people to recruit. This, Taozen says, is when the trouble started. In 1998, Taozen's father was badly beaten, and his older brother was shot dead by the Taliban for the family's weapons. Taozen's parents were terrified that he might be next. It was as though, Taozen says, his life hung in the balance. Taozen's father told him that he could not lose another son. Taozen's father sold parts of the family's land, and together with their savings, this was enough to raise the thousands of US dollars needed to pay a smuggler, as Taozen put it, 'just to save his life.' It was not uncommon for Hazaras to save, sometimes for as long as four years, to raise the smugglers' fee.

Events in the interim only confirmed the danger. In August 1998, the Taliban attacked the town of Mazar-i-Sharif, the last major city holding out against the Taliban's rule. After an initial, indiscriminate attack, Taliban militiamen methodically searched from house to house for Hazara men of fighting age. Their appearance gave them no way to hide. Hazara men and boys were gunned down in front of their families, their bodies left out in front of their houses for the families to see. The Taliban massacred approximately 2000 Hazaras over the course of three days, as they took over the city.

When your life is hanging in the balance

When your life is hanging in the balance, you have no choice but to run. They shot my elder brother, they tried to recruit me as a child soldier, that's a major thing, a huge event. I was very young when I left, only 20 years of age, it was the family who made the decision to get me out of the country because I am the second in line. We did not have enough money to take the whole family out. My father found somebody who was doing some work trafficking humans and left with me out of the country, to the neighbouring country, Pakistan, in a ute, covered at the back. Generally they used it for smuggling goods. When they took goods, sometimes, they smuggled people. The smugglers were generally Pashtun people, our neighbours. They had links to the Taliban. When they were stopped at the border, they would say in their language, 'I'm just taking these goods.' Sometimes they would give them money so they don't check. Because every few kilometres there was a checkpoint – warlords. I did not have many belongings with me. I brought a cassette tape and a small carrying bag with my clothing and some dried fruit, and things like that.

For as long as there have been established smuggling routes, it would seem, smugglers have made little distinction between things and people.

The smugglers had network links, they took us to the airport, they knew how to clear the airport, to get you on the plane. And from there you went to another country, and there are more people there who pick you up from the airport.

As he set out on what was to be the riskiest and loneliest journey of his life, Taozen did not know where he was going, or what his final destination would be. His first stop was Quetta, in Pakistan. Here, he was locked in a house for two weeks with a couple of other Hazaras, while the smugglers organised Pakistani passports and ID cards. In Quetta, too, being Pashtun made it easier to organise false documents. Taozen, who was away from his family and alone for the first time in his life, was afraid. But his journey had only just begun. Taozen took his first ever trip on an aeroplane when he was flown from Pakistan to Indonesia. Here, he and the other Hazaras were met by new smugglers. The people smugglers had their own networks. They worked across borders in cooperation, and sometimes sold a job – and the people involved – to another smuggler. From the airport in Indonesia, he was taken to a private home, where he met more Hazaras, and Afghanis. Taozen spent a few weeks in Indonesia, being moved from house to house, and from Jakarta, to Bali, to Lombok.

Let me die freely

One night the smugglers came. Taozen and the others were told to hurry. They were loaded into four-wheel drives and taken to the beach. It was dark, and everyone had to be quiet. At the beach on Lombok, two small fishing boats had been made ready. They boarded quickly, and were taken below deck. Covers were placed over the decks, so that the passengers could not be seen from the air. When the sun came up, Taozen found himself at sea, for the first time in his life.

Fearful that they would be deserted, the passengers organised for people to do night shifts, staying awake to keep watch on the Indonesian sailors on whom their lives now depended.

The boat trip took 12 nights and 12 days. There were around 40 people, mostly men and kids. There was big engine noise, smoky fumes coming out, it was damp as well, it was quite scary, pitch black, cramped up together. I felt very seasick. After a couple of nights and days I came out, throwing up, feeling very sick. I decided I'm not going to stand it anymore. If I die, let me die freely. So I went to the bow of the boat and sat there with my friends. One night it was very rough, the sea was rough, everything was wobbly, waves a few metres, falling on top of us. We were just waiting and hoping and praying that we were going to make it. There were not a lot of safety vests, there was no GPS, no satellite phone, there was nothing. Food was very scarce, there were a few noodles and things like that for us. That night was very scary. Everyone was praying, people were crying, thinking about their family, things like that. Ten of us were in the bow of the boat, holding hands. I couldn't swim.

For a whole night we were like that. There was water leaking in the boat, people throwing it out. Very chaotic. We spent the whole night [awake]. It was scary. We had some plastic cushions that we put underneath us. So we put them on top of us, for shelter from the water. Around morning I went to sleep. When I woke up the sun was out, and I saw the sea was calm and we were moving.

After 12 days and nights a plane flew over us, just checking something. It came very low, so it could see us. They did a couple of rounds and flew off. And then we saw a navy ship coming towards us, a big ship. We were going very slowly. We saw a small boat coming down from the navy ship. There were a couple of commandos with machine guns. They had semi-automatic weapons, they told us to put our hands up. 'Don't move!' A couple of them jumped on our boat. We had our hands up, waiting there. There was a doctor and an engineer on the boat, they spoke English. They checked over the boat. Slowly we were moved from our boat to the navy ship, and we were sitting at the back of the navy ship with a couple of guards here and there. And they towed the boat. It took a day and a half before we came to Broome.

Taozen arrived in Australia in 1999. He and the others were driven two hours north to Curtin Detention Centre, on an RAAF base, about 40 kilometres south of the town of Derby, in the Kimberley, in Australia's far northwest. The camp was surrounded by two layers of razor wire. Taozen remembers heat, remoteness and a lot of trees. Exhausted and stressed, Taozen was not mistaken. Curtin is extraordinarily remote, situated in one of the most sparsely inhabited regions in the world. Derby, the closest town, has a population of just over 3000, and is one of only three towns in the Kimberley to have a population of more than 2000. When Taozen and his fellow travellers arrived, the camp had only recently been opened. It was, as the government of the time acknowledged, the most primitive of the country's processing centres. It was certainly the most difficult to access.

There were four blocks at Curtin, labelled A–D. Taozen was in block C, and he was given a number that replaced his name, and which was used for food, medication and visits to the doctor. Fifty of them came to Curtin together, and there were 50 people already at the camp. When there were no more than 200–300 people in the camp, Taozen says, they were quite comfortable there. They were well cared for, and there was plenty of food. But the numbers in the camp soon swelled to 1000, and things became very different. Life became very harsh. There were no toiletries or medication. Taozen says that when people visited the doctor, they were told to 'drink plenty of water,' and they would be fine. The camp only lasted three years, closing in 2002 after unrest and rioting by those who had been taken there.

When Taozen left his family, and was driven away in the back of a truck, he had no idea where he would be taken. He did not know that Australia, a distant land about which he knew nothing, was to be his final destination. All he knew was that his father had paid for him to go somewhere safe. Taozen had never been on a plane, and had never seen the sea. He spent three months in Curtin Detention Centre. Each day, he says, felt like a month. He was not able to contact his family.

You're on your own from here

In Christmas 1999, the group of men from Taozen's ship were all given refugee status, and granted their Temporary Protection Visa, or TPV. This meant that the Australian Government acknowledged its obligation to protect them. At the same time, though, they could only remain in Australia temporarily, for up to three years, after which time they could apply for another TPV. They were allowed to work and were given access to Medicare. They could not study. If they left the country, they could not return. Nor could they sponsor family members for an Australian visa. For Taozen, the TPV was a piece of paper, and being granted it was to be told 'see you later, you're on your own from here'. Taozen's initial experience of life in Australia was isolating and frightening. Away from family and his community, he was scared that he would lose his language, his culture, and thus his identity. He found it very difficult to adjust. But notwithstanding the challenges, Taozen felt he could be certain of one thing: the Taliban was not going to kill him in Australia.

When Taozen and the others were granted their TPV, they were told they could settle in Brisbane, Adelaide or Tasmania. Taozen chose Brisbane, along with 20 others. But Taozen could not find a job in Brisbane, so, after a couple of months, he moved to Melbourne. In Melbourne, Taozen found a Hazara man living in the suburb of Dandenong, 30 kilometres from the city centre, a highly multicultural suburb, where only 23 per cent of the population speak English at home. This man helped Taozen to find a place to live and a job in a factory. But Taozen is a proud Hazara. Hazaras are said to differ from other groups in Afghanistan because of their progressive attitude to education. For Hazaras, education has always been the way out of marginalisation, and so they have tended to seek out and take up opportunities. They are disproportionately represented in formal education, and women are not discriminated against. This egalitarian approach to gender roles where education is concerned was one of the many reasons the Taliban found to attack them. In Australia, Taozen studied English wherever and as much as he could. When the free classes ran out, he used his earnings to pay for classes. And then he began to study, and to gain qualifications.

In 2000, Taozen's father moved the whole family out of Afghanistan. They crossed the border into Pakistan and settled in a city with a large Hazara community. In 2001, his father returned to Afghanistan to finalise the sale of their possessions there. He never returned, and the family do not know what fate befell him. Now Taozen's family consists of one brother and sister, still in Pakistan – Taozen's mother and one sibling died a few years ago. One of Taozen's brothers also came to Australia on a UN-sponsored plan and joined Taozen in Melbourne in 2013. Taozen was given permanent residency in Australia in 2005, and as soon as he was able, he flew to Pakistan to see his family. He sends money when he can.

Hazaras are still discriminated against. The Taliban was removed from power in Afghanistan after the American-led invasion in 2001. But they were not defeated. Hazaras in Afghanistan are caught in the middle of fighting that still goes on between rival fundamentalist groups. They are regularly abducted and murdered. A vehicle will be stopped at a checkpoint, the Hazara identified, and captured, tortured or executed on the spot, by the side of the road. In November 2015, seven Hazaras were beheaded in the south of the country. One of the victims was a nine-year-old child, along with adults from Taozen's village. Seventeen years after the Western invasion, Ghazni was once again under attack by Taliban forces. Before dawn on 10 August 2018, Taliban fighters stormed the city. Afghan security forces were killed, and communications were cut.

Taozen is active as an advocate for his community, for refugees and for multiculturalism. In refugee advocacy, Taozen has met many other refugees. On one occasion, when Taozen described to a fellow refugee all that he had done, this man's response was to call him an entrepreneur. Taozen had never heard the term before. But when he found out its meaning, he took it on for himself. An entrepreneur takes risks, he told me, and that is what he had been doing since he left Afghanistan. 'People coming by boat, they are already entrepreneurs.' Taozen, proud Australian, proud Hazara; entrepreneur.

11

LENA HATTOM:
COMING TO AUSTRALIA ON THE *SIEV-IV*.
ONE FAMILY'S JOURNEY

with Ruth Balint

In 2001, Nahar Sobbi and her four children boarded a boat in southeast Indonesia to take them to Australia. Their boat, the Olong, *sank in the Timor Sea. It was the boat at the centre of the Children Overboard Affair, an incident that became infamously associated with the Howard Government's cynical appropriation of refugee boat crossings to demonise asylum seekers during the lead-up to the 2001 federal election. Lena Hattom, a relative, interviewed Nahar and her eldest son Emin in 2009. She discovered that this terrifying ordeal was only one chapter in a two-year odyssey of flight from Iraq.*

In 1985, Nahar flew from Baghdad to Dubai to meet her fiancé, Besam, a Mandaean who had left Iraq and was working in the United Arab Emirates as a jeweller. Nahar was 25 years old. She and Besam married, and had four children: Emin in 1989, Yasmin in 1993, and Adam and Yehya, twins, in 1996. An English literature graduate, Nahar worked as a medical interpreter in a large, busy hospital.

The Sobbi family belong to an ancient sect called the 'Mandaeans', or 'Sabian-Mandaeans'. It is widely believed that Mandaeanism is one of the oldest monotheistic religions in the Middle East and the oldest surviving gnostic religion on earth. Their language is Aramaic.

The Mandaean people were persecuted in Saddam Hussein's Iraq. This was no doubt exacerbated by the tenets of their religion, which emphasise pacifism and non-violence, even in self-defence. A 2008 report released by a Mandaean human rights group noted that there had been increasing attacks against their community by both radical Islamists and the Saddam Hussein regime, as well as ongoing structural discrimination in all areas of life.[1] These conditions forced approximately 15 000 Mandaeans to flee from Iraq during Saddam's reign, the Sobbi family among them.

In 1999, after 14 years in Dubai, Nahar and Besam decided to visit Iraq and their only remaining relative there, Besam's sister. It would be the first time their children would see the country of their parents. They flew to Jordan and rented a car in order to drive from Amman to Fallujah, as flying was banned by a US- and UK-imposed no fly zone across southern and northern Iraq at this time. At the border, however, Besam was arrested and taken away by Saddam's secret police, and the police also confiscated the passports of Nahar and her children. At that time, those who lived and worked overseas, like the Sobbis, were regarded with suspicion. Besam was detained and tortured. After 21 days without word, Nahar managed to escape back into Jordan with the help of Besam's cousins in Fallujah. Besam was finally released after signing a document in which he agreed to cooperate with the Iraqi Government in any intelligence activities. After gaining his freedom, he promptly escaped to Jordan to join his family.

Many Iraqis fearing persecution are known to have slipped across the border to Jordan, where the government allowed them to remain for up to six months, after which they had to return to Iraq or depart to a third country in order to renew their visa.

Besam knew that living in Iraq was never again an option for their family. Although their lives in Dubai were comfortable, they were far from secure – as foreigners, they were not entitled to permanent residency. Nahar and Besam decided that he ought to go to Sydney, where Nahar's parents, and several of her siblings and their families had settled into a community of around 4000 Mandaeans.[2] They decided it was safer if Besam went alone, claimed asylum, and then sponsored the rest of the family. Besam contacted people smugglers in Jordan, and paid them US$10 000; in return, they gave him a fake passport with a photo of a man similar in appearance to Besam, with some minor modifications. Once he had shaved his head and applied subtle make-up, Besam boarded a plane bound for Australia. When he arrived, he tore up his passport and claimed asylum.

Unfortunately for Besam and his family, shortly before he arrived, Australian immigration laws were changed fundamentally by the Howard Government, as part of a swathe of deterrence measures against asylum seekers. On 20 October 1999, Immigration Minister Philip Ruddock introduced the Temporary Protection Visa (TPV), which restricted refugee access to settlement services. Most importantly for the Sobbi family, it barred family reunion, meaning that refugees already resident in Australia could no longer sponsor their immediate family to join them.

Had Besam and his family known of this legislative change, they would have reassessed their strategy. But the news did not reach Besam until he had arrived at Villawood Detention Centre in Sydney. Nahar was shocked when she heard. She and her children were still stuck in Jordan. Nahar's first priority was the safety of her children and she decided that she had to take matters into her own hands. She knew asylum seekers were arriving in Australia by boat. In every phone call from her husband in the detention centre, he would tell her of each new boat arrival. Besam told his wife, somewhat in jest: 'The day you and the children come by boat, I will prepare a cable and fix it to the electricity. If you sink in the ocean I will kill myself immediately.' She knew it was a 'crazy decision', but she was desperate. They had no family in Jordan. Nahar felt Saddam's spies were everywhere. Nahar was soon met in Jordan by her sister Leila and her three children who had also fled Iraq. They spent the next three months in Jordan, and money was extremely tight. They found cheap accommodation in Amman in one of its roughest neighbourhoods, and Nahar never let her children out of her sight.

Neither the Jordanian Government nor the UNHCR considered Jordan to be a permanent country of asylum. Third-country resettlement is therefore the only durable solution for the overwhelming majority of those whom the UNHCR recognises as refugees in Jordan. Many are not registered as refugees, but instead are undocumented and illegal, living a clandestine and desperate existence. A report by the United States Committee for Refugees and Immigrants (USCRI), written at the time that Nahar and her children were hiding out in Jordan as refugees, found that many Iraqis were among the poorest in Jordanian society, eking out meagre existences in such jobs as street vendors and living in overcrowded and, at times, unsanitary conditions.[3]

During this time, Nahar made contact with a Mandaean people smuggler, and soon obtained passports for her and her children to replace those that had been confiscated in Iraq. In early 2000, the smugglers instructed her and her sister's family, along with several other families (around 50 Mandaeans all together) to board a plane to Malaysia. When they arrived in Kuala Lumpur, the Mandaeans were put up in a hotel and told to lay low. Finally, in the middle of one night several weeks later, they were taken by bus to a secret location, where, they were told, they would be boarding a boat to

Indonesia. But when they arrived at the wharf, they were met by a squad of Malaysian police officers, who promptly demanded to see their passports. The police had received a tip-off as a result of a rivalry between smugglers. The families were herded onto army trucks and transported to a Malaysian detention centre.

The detention centre was enormous, comprising several blocks, each one separated by barbed wire, made entirely of wood and in dilapidated condition. Mosquitoes and sewage were everywhere. One block was for women and children, where Nahar, Leila, and their children were detained. In the next block were the men, including Leila's husband and another relative who had joined the group in Malaysia. Being separated meant that they had to be resourceful to communicate: the families cleverly pushed notes into a bottle cap and flicked them over the fence. Sometimes, if the children asked, the guards would indulge the boys by letting them leave their block and go to the men's block to see their father and uncle. However, the boys also discovered that the blocks were connected by a stormwater drain; when the guards refused, the boys would sneak into the block by crawling through the drain and under the fence. Emin, Nahar's eldest son, preferred the company of the men, since the women were often crying in fear and despair, while the men played cards and told stories to distract themselves. He kept himself occupied by learning the art of killing and hunting geckos, which were everywhere.

Illegal entry and stay in Malaysia is criminalised and migrants often serve time in prisons before being transferred to one of the 12 administrative 'immigration depots' while awaiting deportation. It is thought that this is where Nahar and her family were kept, before being deported out of the country after three weeks.

Nahar was deported with her children back to the United Arab Emirates (UAE), but Leila and her family had no choice but to return to Jordan, and the families were again separated. Nahar stayed in the UAE for a month with her brother-in-law, before leaving to try to get to Australia again to be reunited with Besam. This time, Nahar decided that the safest option was to enter Indonesia under the guise of a tourist visa. She obtained one for Indonesia and another for Thailand, to lend their 'holiday' more legitimacy. In March 2000 they boarded a plane to Indonesia with Brunei Airlines, stopping over in Brunei en route to Jakarta. This time, they made it as far as Indonesia, landing in Jakarta. As they handed their papers over to the customs official, one of Nahar's young twins, Adam, suddenly pleaded with his mother to go to the bathroom. She asked him if he could wait but he was adamant. When they returned, the officer looked once more at their passports, this time more carefully. He asked Nahar about the intention of their visit, to which Nahar answered 'tourist'. But it turned out that Nahar had been given a 16-day working visa instead of a 30-day tourist visa. She became visibly nervous, and the officer increasingly suspicious. He refused to let them enter Indonesia. They were to be deported back to Brunei, from where they had initially boarded their connecting flight.

After spending a day in the transit area of Brunei airport, they caught a plane to Bangkok, their Thailand tourist visas in hand. Money was still scarce but Nahar bought a cheap electric wok, which they snuck into their hotel room and hid from the staff. Emin remembers that his mother 'would cook *everything* in it. Eggs in the morning, she would make *margeh* [Iraqi stew] and *simech* [fish] for lunch, she would make pizza. She would bake *klecha* [an Iraqi date pastry] and then for dessert she would make us jello. All in the one wok. We used to call it the Magic Wok.' Nahar even used the wok to bake bread.

The Sobbis spent three months in Thailand. Their visas expired midway, so they crossed the border into Cambodia in order to obtain a re-entry visa for another 60 days in Thailand. But after the three months were over, the family had to return to Jordan, where they were reunited with Leila and her family. The children attended school for the first time in over a year, as Nahar attempted to return some semblance of stability and normality to their lives. Schooling in Amman was a challenge. Bullies and knife fights were a daily occurrence. Emin, who was a well-behaved, bookish type was threatened and beaten up at school on several occasions by gangs of Jordanian boys.

When the Sobbi family's visas expired they joined the ranks of Iraqis who were undocumented de facto refugees living in Amman, in constant fear of deportation and without any kind of government assistance. The family lived in an apartment in a suburb called Al-Hashimi Al Shamali. The apartment building was owned, and in some parts occupied, by a family of high-ranking police officers with whom Nahar and her children became close. This quelled some of Nahar's fears of deportation, and their support was a welcome relief. But staying in Jordan was never an option. This time Nahar uncharacteristically asked her two eldest children what they wanted. She felt they had been through too much, and if they wanted to stay in Jordan, that was where they would stay. The children were divided. Yasmin wanted to try again. Emin didn't. He was afraid that they would be caught again. However, even he knew that their family had no real future in Jordan, and he missed his father, so they decided to give it another shot.

Nahar made contact with people smugglers in Amman once more, and was again instructed to board a plane to Malaysia, from where they would get a visa for entry to Indonesia from the Indonesian Embassy. But first, there was the issue of the red deportation stamp in Nahar's passport. She placed her passport in the washing machine. At the end of the cycle the passport came out damaged and, most importantly, without the red ink. She then went to the Iraqi Embassy and applied for a new passport, on the premise that she had accidentally placed it in the wash. She was promptly issued with a new one.

So, nine months after they had returned to Jordan for a second time, Nahar and her children boarded another plane to Malaysia, where they were able to get visas for Indonesia, and take a small Lion Air propeller plane to Jakarta. This time, by a small miracle, they made it past customs. They were met by a smuggler in Jakarta airport as arranged, who took them to a small village, where they were left outside a small house. Here they were told to wait. This house was already inhabited by another Mandaean family, also waiting to board a boat to Australia. The house was falling apart and had only one source of electricity, a very dim light in the evening, and food was hard to come by. Emin constructed a trap, and attempted to catch birds. Once, he caught a pigeon, which his mother then defeathered and cooked for their lunch, sharing between the two families. They had no notion of how long they would be kept in the house. Nahar was constantly questioning whether money spent on lunch today would mean that down the track they would be stuck without a cent.

It was during this time that Nahar's loneliness and the struggle of their ordeal finally caught up with her. She became depressed, and distrustful of the other Mandaean family, who had been living under Saddam for the past decade, while she had been living away. She felt completely alone. She could not talk to her husband about what they were experiencing because he would cry on the phone. Nahar couldn't speak openly to her children either. They were too young. She began to talk to herself and was soon talking indiscriminately. 'I talk to the ants. I talk to the clouds. I talk to the plants. Because I don't have anyone to talk to, and I can't talk to the children.' Her children knew that there was something wrong, particularly her eldest son, but she would try to reassure them that they should remain positive and would see their father soon.

They stayed waiting in the house for two months, until one day both families were given two options. There was a boat with a smuggler they had heard of already: Abu Bedir, whose boat was leaving soon.

Or there was another boat with a different smuggler: Abu Quassey, whose boat was leaving some time after. She was asked to choose. 'I went to the garden and I talked to all the plants there,' she remembers. After two hours, Nahar decided to go with Abu Bedir. She contacted the smuggler and informed him of her choice. In hindsight, this was a life-saving decision. Abu Quassey is now in jail for his involvement with the boat that became known as the *SIEV-X*, or Suspected Illegal Entry Vessel X, which sank and took with it hundreds of lives.

Abu Bedir told her to get ready to leave immediately. There was a car coming in ten minutes to pick up passengers. It was evening and as they approached the arranged pick-up location, they met another family whose faces were covered with veils. She initially thought they were Muslim but in fact they were Mandaeans being inconspicuous. Both families knew that as Iraqis in Indonesia their intentions were clear to any person who recognised them.

The families were then taken to another house, 'even filthier than the first', as Nahar recalled. The water was undrinkable and although Nahar had bottled water she believes the children may have swallowed some of it while brushing their teeth, as they soon contracted dysentery. All four were beset with severe diarrhoea, vomiting and high fever. The next day they had to go on the boat, so Nahar contacted a local doctor who gave the children injections. At five o'clock the next morning they were awakened by a knock on the door. They were the only family not yet on the bus. Nahar quickly grabbed her children, still in their pyjamas, and ran to the bus. It was rickety, old and wooden, and Nahar remembers sitting on the bus at dawn watching all the Indonesians rising and heading to the mosque for their morning prayer. She had no idea where they were headed, or whether or not they were going to be taken somewhere and killed.

When they finally arrived at the wharf, they saw a boat that all too closely matched the condition of the bus they had just gotten off. Nahar and several of the others cried out to the smugglers in disbelief that this boat would ever be able to take them all the way across the Timor Sea. The smugglers reassured them: this was not the boat that would take them to Australia but a ferry to transport them to another ship that was much larger and modern, and had comfortable individual cabins for each family. They boarded the *Olong*, a 20-metre wooden boat that now carried 223 passengers and crew. The boat set sail and the sky darkened. Still there was no ship with its individual cabins. The children's clothes were dirty as a result of the dysentery and Yasmin quickly developed seasickness.

Many of those who boarded the boats had already been declared genuine refugees in need of resettlement by the Indonesia-based United Nations High Commissioner for Refugees. Some were known to have waited in Indonesia for over two years for a response from Australian Immigration authorities.

It soon became clear that there was no other boat. Nahar is still haunted by the purple colour of the sea at night, when the water merges with the sky and they become indistinguishable. The boat was rocking wildly and as it plunged from one side to the other, Nahar was certain it would sink. They endured a night of storms, and in the morning, they saw an aeroplane overhead – an RAAF P-3C Orion. People aboard the boat were shouting with joy. Then an Australian Navy vessel, the HMAS *Adelaide*, arrived. Nahar reached for one of the toys which the children had brought – a magnetic drawing board, and laughing with joy, wrote 'We are from Iraq'. The children and their mother broke out into song. 'Go east, go west, Australia is the best.'

The Olong *became known as the* SIEV-IV, *the fourth suspected illegal vessel to have arrived in Australian waters since the Howard Government implemented its border protection regime. Two months earlier, the*

MV Tampa *had performed its famous rescue of the 433 passengers aboard the* Palapa. *The new legislation meant anyone who arrived by boat could no longer apply for permanent residency, or apply for family reunion. Refugee boats were to be turned back before reaching land.*

The naval crew on board the *Adelaide* told the boat to stop, using a megaphone, but a return to Indonesia almost certainly meant Indonesian jail and deportation for the passengers. Commander Norman Banks, the officer in charge of the *Adelaide,* had one instruction: to use every reasonable means to prevent *SIEV-IV* from reaching Christmas Island.[4] After repeated instructions to the *Olong* to halt its journey towards Christmas Island, the *Adelaide* fired 23 rounds of warning shots into the water in front of the *Olong.* The boat's engine was probably wrecked by passengers desperate to be taken on board the Australian boat, rather than be turned back. The *Adelaide* attempted to tow the boat back towards Indonesia by attaching ropes to its hull, but this cemented the damage. The navy dropped food and life-jackets for the passengers. As they approached Nahar she pleaded with them: 'Please don't do it. Don't let me die with my children.' Another night passed in which the boat began to sink.

Throughout the next 24 hours, the boat's condition steadily deteriorated. By 4.30 pm the next day, 8 October, water was coming in over the freeboard. Naval personnel again boarded the boat and attempted to fix the engine, with no success. A pump brought over from the Adelaide *proved useless. Still the passengers were not rescued. Meanwhile, water continued to flood the boat. It was only when the boat had fully sunk that the passengers were finally rescued by Australian officers. Later, Commander Banks would tell the Senate Inquiry into a Certain Maritime Incident that he considered himself 'unashamedly apolitical', but had found himself caught between navy protocol and the highly charged politics of border control.*

Before the water level reached halfway up Nahar's waist, the children aboard the ship, including a three-week-old baby, were rescued from the boat and taken aboard jet boats onto the HMAS *Adelaide*. Adam and Yehya were among these children while Emin managed to swim to HMAS *Adelaide* himself. Nahar and Yasmin were left together on the sinking boat, but Nahar didn't know her three sons were safe. She tried to make contact with her sons in this moment: 'We used to, when they were children if they are lost – I used to make this ... you know "'ello!" to call them – from Pingu [a children's cartoon]. So whenever we travel, whenever we go to shopping centres, if I lost them and I make "'ello!" and they make "'ello!", I know they are safe and they know [where I am] and we can come together. So I'm in the middle of the ocean and I start to call "'ello"!' But there was no reply. Yasmin took her mother's hand and helped her through the water within the safety of shark nets. To this day Nahar claims that her daughter saved her life.

Once they reached HMAS *Adelaide* the asylum seekers climbed the steep ladder to the top of the ship. They were freezing cold and wet. The moment Nahar reached the deck she searched for her sons, and to her relief found them dressed in oversized navy overalls. Soon all the asylum seekers were aboard the navy ship and were being given hot meals. Still, Emin's dysentery persisted for five days. 'He became like a stick; diarrhoea, vomiting, and no treatment.' Nahar was continually changing his overalls, as they each became soiled. There was a doctor on board who was able to give Emin some medicine, but his condition still did not improve.

Meanwhile, senior ministers in the Howard Government told Australians, untruthfully, that asylum seekers had thrown their children into the water. Children who had been held up by their parents to show that children were on board and help was needed, was instead misconstrued as parents threatening to throw their children overboard.

Immigration Minister Philip Ruddock publicly stated: 'I regard these as some of the most disturbing practices I've come across in public life.' John Howard's own stance on the issue was just as blunt: 'I don't want people like that in Australia.' The media, however, demanded proof of the incident. After much scrambling and delay, Canberra produced photographs taken during the rescue of the passengers of the sinking Olong *by naval officers. Fortunately for the Howard Government, the truth was not to surface publicly until after election day.*

The *Olong* passengers circled Christmas Island for three days, after which they were finally able to land. Buses arrived at the beach and transported them to a large gymnasium, like an indoor basketball court. There were Goanna stretcher beds set up for them to sleep on. The next day Nahar begged officials for medical attention for Emin, who was looking increasingly frail with his persistent dysentery. They took Nahar and her son to the hospital, and ran some tests. Emin remained in the hospital for four days until his condition stabilised.

Back in the gymnasium the asylum seekers were informed that they would be taken somewhere to be processed. They were then herded onto Hercules military aircrafts that had been stripped of their insides. For six hours they sat in the plane with the engine roaring, in freezing temperatures, wearing nothing but the shorts and t-shirts they had been given on Christmas Island. They were given earmuffs but these had little impact, as the plane was intended only for lightweight military use and had no insulation. Nahar placed the paper vomit-bags on their exposed feet in order to provide some warmth, again with little effect.

The plane finally landed on what Nahar and the asylum seekers had assumed would be Australian land. They were surprised, however, to see that all the people around them were dark-skinned and living in what they thought of as a jungle. Where were they? Nahar then remembered Besam mentioning that Australia had planned to rent

Papua New Guinea (PNG). She realised that this was where they had landed, and told the other puzzled asylum seekers. On Manus Island, the asylum seekers were taken to a group of old war bunkers, essentially empty domes with only old bunk beds inside. They were then handed mosquito nets. Malaria was rife on the island. Nahar asked for some mosquito repellent and applied it to her children and herself. Finally, the Sobbi family lay down under the mosquito net, covered in the lotion, and slept.

This was a strange time for their family. While on Manus Island they were fenced off from the locals, who would approach the gates and ask the asylum seekers for food or money. When they asked the government officials why they needed to be fenced off they were told that the island had a history of cannibalism, and that it was for their own safety. Temperatures were stifling, and sleeping in the dome bunkers (which had no ventilation) was virtually impossible. Finally, Nahar decided that they should move their beds out of the bunkers and sleep outdoors with the nets draped over them. Soon many of the other asylum seekers followed suit and the domes became empty. After several months of sleeping outside, air-conditioned caravans were brought in. The bathroom and toilets did not have any doors, so Nahar took sheets from the bunkers and strung them up like curtains. Women were also using the sheets to make clothes for their children, as all their belongings had disappeared into the ocean along with the *Olong*.

Nahar remembers that one of the most subtle, yet difficult aspects of this time on Manus Island was that each asylum seeker was referred to by a number. Yasmin can still recite each family member's numbers off by heart. Nahar felt that her identity was being killed. One saving grace within this experience however, was a friendship that formed between herself and one of the representatives of the International Organization for Migration (IOM), a lawyer by the name of Virginia. Virginia conducted short interviews with all the asylum seekers, and then helped them to make contact with their families. The night before the Sobbis left Jordan for the last time, Nahar had asked each of her children to memorise a phone number. Emin hadn't been able to, but Yasmin had been more conscientious. Finally they were able to make contact with their family and let them know that they were safe. Virginia interviewed Nahar again in November 2001 in order to assess her application. Nahar recalls that as she was interviewed and told her story, Virginia was weeping. She told Nahar that she didn't know what to tell her – but that she would help her.

The Manus Island Regional Processing Centre was established in 2001 along with the Nauru Regional Processing Centre as an 'offshore processing centre', part of the Pacific Solution policy created by the Howard Government. At this time, the Sobbi family's claim for asylum was able to be processed while they were on Manus.

The greatest challenge of all for the Sobbis was the other Muslim refugees. Several of them were suspicious of the family from the outset, and that suspicion only increased on Manus Island. Because of their English skills and their Western demeanour, they were often a sole point of contact between the asylum seekers and government officials or the IOM representatives. This contact inevitably led to suspicions that the Sobbis were receiving preferential treatment. In addition, Nahar believes that being a single woman as well as a Mandaean made her a target. Nahar endured verbal and physical abuse and was often blamed for anything that went wrong.

During their nine-month detention on Manus Island, the Sobbis also began to learn more about the Mandaean faith. They had never been religious, and knew almost nothing about it. Among the asylum seekers, however, was a religious Mandaean man, and he began to teach them about their history, beliefs and the prayers. The Mandaean Association, based in Sydney's Liverpool, discovered there were

Mandaeans detained on Manus Island and sent over a parcel with several Mandaean holy books (including the Ginza, the core text of the faith). Emin took this religious schooling particularly seriously. He would wake up at dawn to recite prayers which he memorised. He learned how to read and write in Aramaic, and he performed a daily baptism. Every spare moment Emin had was spent reading from the Ginza.

The IOM also brought English books for the Sobbi children to read, as well as board games such as Pictionary. The new detention facilities were being built around them and soon the asylum seekers had access to a television and were able to eat in a proper dining area. The Sobbis also began to work: Nahar as an interpreter in the medical clinic, Emin and Yasmin in the kitchen. In return for their work the Sobbis were paid in vouchers, which they could redeem in phone calls to Besam. They called him nearly every day. The IOM also provided the smokers in the group with cigarettes. Nahar would smoke less so that she could sell her surplus cigarettes to the PNG locals for American dollars. By the time Nahar left the PNG detention centre she had over US$400.

Towards the end of the Sobbis' time on Manus Island, the IOM also started a small school. There were two classes: one for the younger children with drawing and craft activities, and another for the older children with English classes. The IOM built a playground and a library, and established knitting classes so that the older ladies in the group could share their skills with asylum seekers who wished to learn. Soccer and chess tournaments were held. Unlike most of the asylum seekers who had never seen a computer, Emin and Yasmin had significant technical skills, and so IOM established a computer room where the two Sobbi children ran computer classes. The IOM even provided special food for the Mandaeans to celebrate their religious new year; the *Karsa*. Women made their own yoghurt and baked their own bread in a *tannour* (clay oven) that they had constructed at the camp. As the IOM began to trust the asylum seekers more, they allowed them to light fires and this enabled them to start doing what many of the Arab women loved to do: cook.

One day, five long months after their interviews, the IOM officials gathered the asylum seekers together. They announced that every single asylum seeker's application had been successful. Nahar and the asylum seekers just stood there silently as if they had heard nothing, anticipating a catch, something worse. The Egyptian interpreter translated, but still they did not understand that they had been accepted. Finally the interpreter shouted at them 'Hey! Wake up! Your applications – all of you – have been accepted!' Nahar almost fainted and remembers that several people came and held her. Then she began to cry with joy. They were going to Australia. Finally, in mid-2002, the Sobbi family arrived in Sydney where they were reunited with Besam.

In 2003, the Manus Island Regional Processing Centre fell into disuse in preference for the one at Nauru and in 2008, was closed by the Rudd Government. In November 2012, it was reopened by the Labor Government and a year later, boat arrivals were told they would never be allowed to settle in Australia. In 2017 it was formally closed, with hundreds of detainees forced on to the PNG economy.

Since 2002, the family have been living in Sydney's western suburbs, in close proximity to Nahar's parents, and the families of several of her siblings. Each of the children attended school and university, and have since established careers and families. The Sobbi family say they are deeply grateful for the safety and security afforded to them as refugees in Australia.

12

AYE MIN SOE: SHOOTING SOLDIERS

with Julie Kalman

Aye Min Soe is a clever, thoughtful man, with a deep love for his country, and a strong moral compass. He belongs to the Mon ethnic group, one of eight major groups of the 135 so-called 'national races' recognised by the government in multi-ethnic Myanmar.[1] His family were part of the country's political elite. When Burma won its independence from Britain in 1948 after almost six decades of full colonial rule, Aye Min's grandfather was named Minister of Information.

Infected with the protest virus

In 1998, Aye Min received a bachelor's degree in chemical engineering from what was then Rangoon Institute of Technology (it has since changed its name to Yangon Technological University). He calls it his 'parents' degree', because his great passion has always been journalism, and his great interest, history and politics. At university, Aye Min joined the student union. But the Burma in which he lived was ruled by a repressive military regime. This was the State Law and Order Restoration Council, or SLORC (later renamed the State Peace and Development Council). The SLORC was a compromise regime, put in place after the Burma Socialist Programme Party (BSPP) came to an end following widespread protests in 1988. The protests marked the end of 26 years of rule in Burma for General Ne Win, whose 'Burmese Way to Socialism' had made the country one of the most isolated in the world.

The SLORC continued in much the same vein. Order was maintained through violent crackdowns. Elections were held in 1990 and their results ignored, after opposition groups and ethnic parties won 475 of the 485 non-military seats. Senior opposition leaders, including Aung San Suu Kyi, were imprisoned. In 1992, the relatively uneducated and reportedly 'uncharismatic' Senior General Than Shwe came to power. British human rights activist Benedict Rogers has described Shwe as 'one of the world's most brutal and reclusive dictators'.[2] Under General Than Shwe's rule, any dissent was crushed. Students were particularly suspect, of course, and membership of a university student union was illegal. Aye Min joined nonetheless. He was, he tells me, 'infected with the protest virus'. He felt he needed to tell the world about mismanagement, corruption, and human rights abuses happening in Myanmar.

We will shoot soldiers with cameras

It was during his student days that Aye Min co-founded Burma VJ, or Burma video journalists. The impetus behind it, he told me, was the idea that 'soldiers always shoot with guns, so we will shoot them with cameras'. Aye Min travelled the country with a camera, filming undercover. From a small group of fellow-minded students, they built up a network of Burmese expatriates. First, they made contact with an organisation in Norway. This was DVB, or Democratic Voice of Burma, the Myanmar broadcaster in exile. Many of their members had begun at another broadcaster in exile called Student Democratic Force, which operated a small radio station in the dense jungle on the Thai–Myanmar border. Now the footage they shot would be smuggled out of Myanmar, by courier, the internet, and satellite hook-ups, so that it could be edited in Oslo, and screened elsewhere. In the act of filming, Aye Min and his fellow students had made themselves outlaws, and by sending the footage outside Myanmar, they became smugglers.

Aye Min spent five years in jail because of his student activism. He was 21 years old when he was arrested in the countryside, where he had fled to try to escape government forces. Before a military court, he was charged with high treason, a charge that was punishable by death. Aye Min's lawyer appealed the sentence, and it was commuted to five years. He spent three of those years in solitary confinement, in terrible conditions. He was shackled, a widespread practice in Burmese prisons at that time. I put it to Aye Min that he was lucky, in one way, to have been sentenced to 'only' five years. He agrees. Many of his friends were given longer sentences. Some of them are still in prison. He and his other friends who have the good fortune to be free do not know how to help them.

Aye Min came out of prison more determined than ever. He continued to film undercover. He and his fellow student journalists, using the code name Joshua, were filming when, in September 2007, the regime decided to lift subsidies on fuel, doubling the price. People had had enough. In the documentary of the protests, with footage taken by Aye Min and his fellow 'Joshuas', a taxi driver states that he is ready to join whatever demonstrations should erupt. People took to the streets, led by thousands of Buddhist monks, along with students and political activists, in protests that became known as the Saffron Revolution. In late September, the SLORC responded with a harsh crackdown. Several hundred protesters were arrested or detained. Aye Min and others continued filming, capturing the brutal response by the Myanmar authorities, including police beatings, and the shooting, at point-blank range, of a Japanese journalist, Kenji Nagai. They captured the moment when a group of students found themselves surrounded by soldiers, and followed them with the camera as some of the students, chanting they were 'not afraid to die', moved to the front of the demonstration. Little by little, they smuggled this footage out, and this was fed, via Oslo, to CNN and the BBC. Aye Min was indeed letting the world know. As an admiring *New York Times* journalist wrote, 'they not only exposed the totalitarian character of the Myanmar authorities to world scrutiny, they revealed the future of war reporting'.[3]

At the same time, in Denmark, Anders Østergaard, a documentary filmmaker, had been approached by his producer to make a film on Myanmar. He had been put in touch with Democratic Voice of Burma. It was Østergaard who gathered the smuggled footage and put it together as a 90-minute documentary, titled *Burma VJ: Reporting from a Closed Country. Burma VJ* was released in 2008, to enormous acclaim. It won a slew of international awards, including Best Documentary at the European Film Awards, and the Grand Jury Prize at the Sundance Film Festival. The documentary was nominated for an Academy Award for Best Documentary Feature. Given the worldwide publicity they received, it was perhaps inevitable that the Burmese authorities would find out about the activities of Burma VJ. Their office was raided by police. As the documentary made from the footage they had shot was being feted around the world, Aye Min, now married, left his wife and two young sons, and fled to a hiding place in the countryside. He had to stay in Myanmar, because he was still managing the network of undercover journalists shooting soldiers with their hidden cameras, but he could only see his family every few months, knowing that they, too, were being watched and harassed by military intelligence.

Putting on one's best clothes

In early May 2008, Myanmar was hit by the worst natural disaster in its recorded history. This was Cyclone Nargis. The country is prone to natural disasters, exacerbated by the fact that some 70 per cent of Myanmar's population of approximately 55 million live in rural areas, and they are overwhelmingly poor. Myanmar is one of Asia's poorest countries, ranked 148 out of 189 countries and territories in the UN

Development Program. Cyclone Nargis brought high winds and a three-metre storm surge, devastating the region of the Ayeyarwady Delta, a low, densely populated fertile plain, where people lived from rice-growing and fishing. The Red Cross estimates that 84 500 people were killed, with 53 800 missing. The UN estimates that as many as 2.4 million people were affected by the cyclone, which destroyed homes and livelihoods. Help was desperately needed.

But the regime saw international aid organisations as potential threats to internal control. Than Shwe refused visas to organisation staff and refused the right of entry to ships carrying relief supplies. Myanmar citizens who sought to bring relief on their own initiative could be arrested. By 12 May, UN Secretary-General Ban Ki-moon voiced his 'immense frustration' at what he called the 'unacceptably slow' response of the Myanmar regime to the crisis.[4] Aye Min was there, filming in Nargis's aftermath, and continuing to smuggle out footage.

Not long after Nargis, Aye Min's picture was taken when he participated in a protest, and with ever fewer places to hide safely, it was time for him to leave his country. In December 2008, he crossed the border into Thailand. This was not a difficult thing to do. The border that purportedly marks the boundary between the two states is highly porous. There are checkpoints, but as Aye Min explained to me, it is not necessary to show identification in crossing. It is simply a matter of putting on one's best clothes and greeting the border guards with head held high, as though one is on important business, rather than fleeing a hostile regime. His wife and two sons, together with his mother, followed one month later, escaping harassment by the Myanmar military police.

In Thailand, the family settled in Mae Sot, a Thai town that abuts the Myanmar border. Thanks to its position, Mae Sot is a trading hub, and part of its trade is in bodies: many from Myanmar cross the border, whether as refugees or for economic reasons, and settle in Mae Sot. The town is also a notorious location for smuggling. In many ways, it is a typical border town. Smuggling, crime and police bribery are facts of life. Small boats ply their trade, bringing goods back and forth across the Moei River. Early each morning, they bring illegal workers across the river from Myanmar. They return with a load of tax-free Thai goods. The town is a central site for legitimate trade, too. It is a central point in Thailand for jade and gems. The large displaced population from Myanmar has brought new industries to Mae Sot. There are 235 factories, mainly producing garments, and many of those from Myanmar work in these factories, filling low-paid jobs. Their presence, living in Thailand as illegal immigrants, brings humanitarian organisations and their workers to Mae Sot, as well. The Myanmar community there makes up a significant proportion of the population (there is no definite figure for this, although Aye Min's estimate is that 70 per cent of the population of Mae Sot is from Myanmar).

In coming to Mae Sot, Aye Min found himself in a place that was both familiar, and fraught. Mae Sot is Thailand's easternmost town, six kilometres from the border with Myanmar. The town, of approximately 40 000 inhabitants, is in the Tak province. It forms one part of the 2500-kilometre-long border that Thailand and Myanmar share, marked by the long, narrow Moei River. Tak province itself is remote and difficult to access, on steep and winding roads with hairpin bends. It is a vast and mountainous wilderness. National parks adjoin to form one of the largest intact jungles in Southeast Asia. Indigenous hill tribes inhabit the dense jungle that covers the mountains.

Mae Sot, on the other hand, is small, but bustling, and one of the most culturally diverse towns in Thailand. Thais mix with Hmong and Karen from the hill tribes, but above all, the town is a magnet for both refugees and migrants from neighbouring Myanmar. Mae Sot was the location of Myanmar's first land border, opened in 2013. The

Thai–Myanmar Friendship Bridge crosses the border at Mae Sot, and it is the official border checkpoint. But ethnic and political refugees fleeing the SLORC have been crossing into Thailand for decades.

Very good customers

It was in Mae Sot that Aye Min lived with his family for five years. Their two boys studied at an informal school. They were stateless, vulnerable, and in constant danger. They avoided the threat of arrest by offering regular bribes. They were, as he puts it, 'very good customers' for the Thai police, who could make a healthy side living in the town. Agents of the Myanmar military intelligence also circulated in Mae Sot, and it could be difficult to know who to trust. Aye Min was still being watched.

Aye Min and his family had fled immediate danger in Myanmar. But they did not feel a sense of freedom in Thailand. The Thai Government is not a signatory to the 1951 Convention relating to the Status of Refugees, nor to its 1967 Protocol. The 1951 Refugee Convention is a United Nations multilateral treaty. It defines who is a refugee. It sets out the rights of individuals who are granted asylum, and the legal obligations of nations that grant asylum. It builds on the Universal Declaration of Human Rights, which recognises a person's right to seek asylum in another country from persecution in their own. The UNHCR (United Nations High Commissioner for Refugees) oversees the Convention, and its 1967 Protocol. States are expected to cooperate with the UNHCR in applying the Convention. A core principle of the Refugee Convention is non-refoulement; that is, that a refugee should not be returned to a country where they face serious threats to their life or freedom.

The Convention defines a refugee as anyone who, 'owing to well-founded fear of being persecuted for reasons of race, religion, nationality, membership of a particular social group or political opinion, is outside the country of his nationality and is unable or, owing to such fear, is unwilling to avail himself of the protection of that country; or who, not having a nationality and being outside the country of his former habitual residence as a result of such events, is unable or, owing to such fear, is unwilling to return to it'.

There is no formal asylum framework in Thai law. Refugees in Thailand are not covered by the Convention. The Thai state allows them to remain temporarily in Thailand, while awaiting repatriation, or relocation. Refugees in Thailand are considered illegal immigrants, and they have no right to Thai citizenship. (Less than one per cent of asylum seekers from Myanmar are granted refugee status.) They cannot work, and their freedom of movement is limited. They are dependent on humanitarian aid from NGOs for all basic needs.

When Aye Min went to Thailand, the country was playing host to more than two million migrants. It had become increasingly difficult for the UNHCR to implement its mandate there. With the large number of people converging on Thailand, the Thai Government's attention turned to national security and international diplomacy. The principle of asylum did not take precedence. In 2007, Thai authorities requested that the UNHCR stop making refugee status determinations in Thailand. The Thai regime placed restrictions on exit visas, making it more difficult for the UNHCR to organise resettlement for refugees who had been accepted by another country. In other words, the Thai regime shifted from a solution-oriented approach, to deterrence. They sought to make conditions difficult for would-be refugees, so as to stem the flow. The UNHCR is particularly concerned about Myanmar refugees in Thailand, calling their situation 'among the most protracted in the world'. The majority of them have lived in camps for more than two decades. They live in extreme poverty, with the constant threat of arrest and deportation.

How about a passport?

Aye Min and his family had no documentation allowing them to remain in Thailand. They lived with the threat of being deported back to Myanmar. Aye Min knew that this would mean his immediate arrest and imprisonment, and possible death. He had made an application for refugee status, but this had become caught between UN and Thai Government bureaucracy. Like so many asylum seekers from Myanmar, his request had fallen between the cracks of political responsibility. It was to Aye Min's great fortune that he could use his journalism to his advantage.

Aye Min was still pursuing his journalism. The Thai–Myanmar border was – and still is – rife with insurgents, as some of the many ethnic minorities continue to wage the world's longest civil war, particularly against the former, anti-democratic regime. Even with democratisation, there is little or no relief from the violence along the border. These regions are hilly and remote, and thus difficult to control. Student Democratic Force, the organisation with which Burma VJ was in contact, could run its illicit radio station from inside the jungle along the border, which is some of the world's thickest. The jungle provides a haven for Karen insurgents, too. With insurgency, comes crime. Myanmar accounts for one-quarter of the world's opium production, second only in the world to Afghanistan. The cash raised by the drug trade allows rebel groups to buy the weapons they need. Further funds are raised by the illicit trade in jade. In these border regions, insurgents, illegal workers and refugees come together.

Just as with the story recounted in Chapter 1 of smugglers taking desperate Polish Jews across the Bug River, on the Thai–Myanmar border, smugglers diversify. They have contacts in counterfeiting networks, skilled in obtaining fake passports. As a journalist, Aye Min had many connections. He had contacts among insurgents from the border regions between Thailand and Myanmar. Criminals were 'easy to find' in such places. Sometimes, he says, he would interview them, and it was easy to take them aside, turn off the microphone, and ask, 'How about a passport?' Aye Min was able to obtain a proper Myanmar passport, although he was obliged to do this through illegal channels, because, as a wanted man in his own country, he would never have been granted this precious document by the regime. For a little less than A$5000, funds supplied by the Democratic Voice of Burma in Oslo, Aye Min became the holder of a travel and identification document from Myanmar. He was lucky. Criminals operating in border areas were not altruists. Aye Min was known to the insurgent leader, and criminals would not dare to cheat him, for fear of reprisals. When they can cheat people, he told me, they do. He gives the example of Rohingya Muslims, who pay smugglers a great deal of money, thinking that they will be taken to the United States. They end up in Thai refugee camps.

Both are beautiful

Passport in hand, Aye Min first travelled to Denmark, to take part in a conference on the media. More than anything, he wanted the world to know about the abuses taking place in his country. But now, as someone who was legally documented, he was also able to apply for residency, and on his return to Thailand, he submitted applications to the embassies in Bangkok of Norway, the United States, Canada and Australia. After a two-year wait, approval came through from Australia, and in July 2014, Aye Min, his wife, and his two sons, now 11 and 16, were finally able to travel to safety, and a life in Melbourne. Friends who were already here organised a house in Melbourne's outer suburbs, and they provided a network of support. But Aye Min has a mission, and once here, he did not rest. There is a lot of work to do in his country, and this is work that he wants to take on. He is directing all of his studies to this end. His goal is nothing less than national reunification among groups that remain bitterly opposed: the military, civilians and ethnic minority groups. He will have support: some of the students who accompanied and supported Burma VJ during the Saffron Revolution were MPs in Aung San Suu Kyi's government before the military coup. (Many of them, like Aye Min, now live in exile, in the United States, Europe, New Zealand and Canada.) Aye Min has completed a Master's in International Relations, and now he is studying another Master's, in Post-Disaster Project Management. Then, he says, as soon as he is able to obtain Australian citizenship, and thus to travel, he will return to Myanmar. He has an application in the system, and he has been told that this may take another five years. Much of Aye Min's adult life has been spent negotiating hostile bureaucracies.

As we finish, I ask Aye Min if there is anything he would like to add. 'Yes,' he says. He wants me to stress the terrible conditions he endured in prison, a young man of 21, shackled and alone in solitary confinement, for three years. Then his expression changes. 'I married at thirty,' he tells me, with a grin. 'That was my deadline.' Finally, I ask him why he calls his country Burma, not Myanmar. 'Either is fine,' he says. 'Both are beautiful.'

13

THE MULTIPLE FACES OF
THE PEOPLE SMUGGLER

Behrouz Boochani, Claudia Tazreiter
and Omid Tofighian

Behrouz Boochani is well known in Australia and beyond as the award-winning author of No Friend but the Mountains: Writing From Manus Prison. *In his book, Boochani recounts the boat journeys he undertook from Indonesia; journeys of danger and journeys facilitated through smugglers. From 2013 to 2017 Boochani was a political prisoner incarcerated by the Australian Government in the Manus Island Regional Processing Centre (Papua New Guinea) despite having been determined to be a refugee through the 1951 Refugee Convention. Since being forcibly transferred in 2017 he continued to be incarcerated in one of three new prisons (East Lorengau Refugee Transit Centre). Omid Tofighian is a long-time collaborator with Boochani. This contribution emerged through closer links developed when Behrouz Boochani was appointed Adjunct Associate Professor at the University of New South Wales in early 2019, sponsored by Claudia Tazreiter through the Forced Migration Research Network. The authors share a commitment to justice for all people, focused on the most vulnerable and invisible persons.*

Claudia Tazreiter

This chapter reflects on the stigma associated with the label 'people smuggler' and aims to demystify the multiple meanings, identities and emotions behind the label. Our intention is to bring to the fore the invisible and silenced voices, stories and lived reality of people that use smugglers to make journeys to flee violence and persecution. In many cases, these journeys are not possible through usual travel means and routes that require travel documents, visas and interactions with officials and bureaucracies. The stories and the lived experience illuminated in this chapter and throughout this book reappropriates the label 'smuggler' associated with illegal, criminal, nefarious activity, instead clarifying that for refugees and asylum seekers, persons assisting in facilitating journeys out of danger are regularly understood as travel agents, helpers and, sometimes, friends.[1]

For the state, the smuggler is a criminal figure, yet for the 'irregular migrant', the smuggler is someone facilitating a journey. We are interested in the tensions between the language and labels associated with smuggler and irregular migrants, and the social and political consequences of such language and labels. Creating outsiders and enemies occurs socially and politically through generating fear, social distancing and criminalisation.[2] For us, this background is key to unmasking contemporary political and policy interventions in human migrations. In countries such as Australia, understood as a 'settler society' and as an 'immigration nation', the work of nation-building is reflected in high rates of immigration and related wealth creation. Yet, when it comes to the arrival of refugees and asylum seekers, fear and myth-building abound.[3]

The founding myths that accompany colonisation in Australia, as well as its origins as a penal colony, carry significant lessons when reflecting on an Australian national imaginary and the willingness to stigmatise and criminalise certain groups. White Australia was founded on imprisonment, fear and exclusion. The Aboriginal population was typified as a wild, and not fully human enemy. Similarly, these tropes of fear and danger extended to populations to Australia's north with visions of 'Asian hordes' invading without sufficient vigilance (unwanted immigrants). 'White' Australia justified its exclusionary logic and rhetoric through regular reference to these 'wild hordes' from within and from outside the nation state.[4] Such potent tropes of danger and protection leave traces through the treatment of the convict population to the encampment and enslavement of the Indigenous population through settlements, missions, unpaid labour and later the policies of removal of Aboriginal children from their families; all strategies aimed at containment, separation and racialisation. Suspect populations were to be contained, separated from citizens; citizens who were to be kept safe. Indeed, collective memory and the social imaginary in Australia are 'underpinned by feelings of anxiety',[5] and such anxieties are evident in contemporary responses to the claims for visibility by Indigenous people and also by 'irregular migrants' – particularly those travelling by boat and categorised as asylum seekers or refugees – who resist the exercise of state power in detaining, deporting and separating them from citizens. Tropes around people smugglers belong to this categorisation and it is important to remember that often refugees themselves enter into smuggling activities in order to facilitate onward journeys to safety and protection for themselves and their families.

Borders and creating a hierarchy of value attached to persons

The creation and maintenance of a hierarchy of humans through state-instituted practices of segregation and exclusion, relates closely to the multiple meanings and uses of the concept of border.[6] These are problems that appear to be intractable to human societies despite technological, economic and moral development, innovation and 'progress' over generations. Arguably, the very foundations of modernity are deeply implicated in the creation and subsequent exploitation of categorising and applying differential value to people and cultures through colonisation, imperialism as well as racialised capitalism. We see the treatment of refugees and asylum seekers, and by extension the criminalisation of people smugglers, as a manifestation of this injustice.

The voices and experiences of asylum seekers and refugees in the Australian context take exception to the state practices that create hierarchies and differential value attached to persons. The rhetorical and affective messages and moods of danger and of hatred are stark in state practices of criminalising and punishing asylum seekers, often merely for their mode of arrival, by boat. The creation of deterritorialised spaces is evident in Australia's practice of 'off-shore' detention of people seeking asylum on the Pacific island nation of Nauru and on Manus Island, Papua New Guinea – which is akin to Marc Augé's concept of 'non-places',[7] that are also 'spaces of disappearance' as national borders are politicised.[8]

The contemporary traces of racialised exclusion briefly outlined above are able to be traced through past events and processes of exclusion in the practices of encampment, punishment and removal. How can we (refugees and their supporters) challenge and reframe the racialised, ethnicised bodies made into outsiders through intersecting identity markers, race/identity and migration/citizenship status? These links are made visible in the following reflections on people smuggling emerging from a dialogue between Behrouz Boochani and Omid Tofighian.

OMID TOFIGHIAN:

A critical and constructive discussion about the identity and role of people smugglers is fundamental for debordering approaches in migration studies and beyond.[9] Is smuggling a crime or an act of good will? Is it a business or a political venture? Is the objective profit or aid? Are travellers a commodity or are their identities (and futures) meaningful for smugglers?

In our dialogue we aim to identify misleading binaries that underlie many discussions about global human movement; that is, the superficial definitions and polar oppositions integral to border regimes.[10]

A set of politicised dichotomies condition the discourse surrounding people smugglers which reflect broader problems about categories, definitions and theoretical frameworks as bordering practices. More collaborative and multidimensional work is required by scholars and activists to produce a cohesive analysis regarding the identity and role of smugglers, and their networks of operation. Regrettably, the debates have been dominated by politicians and mainstream media and have lacked the nuance and critical reflexivity necessary for initiating transformative work and producing more robust visions of justice. In fact, framing the debate in terms of a dualism has been instrumental in the moral panic pertaining to people smuggling and the subsequent border violence that has ensued. The notion of the people smuggler as criminal and exploiter of human misery has become ubiquitous in political discourse and mainstream media coverage with policies and laws using the language of securitisation and militarisation, and implementing extreme and barbaric measures, to end the practice. Here we argue that people smuggling cannot be neatly located on one side of the dominant dichotomies. Instead, critically engaging with the binaries, understanding the context and limits associated with them, subverts the superficial rhetoric regarding people smuggling and opens spaces for more meaningful and transformative public debate.

Researchers working in the field often face obstacles due to the fact that those within various institutions and groups who receive their work often assume that scholars have made a definitive choice about where they reside in relation to the binaries. That is, the oppositions are understood to be a comprehensive framing of the analytical landscape and also mutually exclusive. There are implicit and explicit demands that one makes an unequivocal choice between conflicting views.

One dichotomy that requires scrutiny is the 'virtuous humanitarian' versus the 'criminal exploiter of misery'. The predominance of criminalisation regarding people smugglers has determined the public debate to such an extent that any diversion from this dominant view is itself relegated to support for criminality and disregard for domestic and international law. This impacts knowledge production pertaining to people smuggling and the way and extent to which research is supported, acknowledged and employed by academics and policy makers. If one refuses to comply with the outright criminalisation of people smugglers, you are then usually required to provide immediate justification for the hardship and sometimes death of people crossing borders through those networks. Is the practice of people smuggling a humanitarian act or a crime? This question has controlled the social imaginary in relation to border politics in ways that cannot be overestimated. Attempting to answer the question quickly reaches an impasse – in fact, both can be correct in some cases and the relationship between the two can take innumerable forms. What is crucial to consider here is that the two concepts do not cancel each other out. A helpful distinction to make here is between the act and the process. In any comparative or analytical critique of people smuggling it is necessary to frame the discussion alongside actions taken by states and international organisations who use money, power and status to determine the movements and circumstances of displaced and exiled peoples. A critical account of people smuggling that singles it out as an exclusive act with its own unique processes fails to acknowledge the way smuggling responds to gross global inequalities and structural discrimination – in some cases smugglers are known to adopt the strategies and tactics of states and international organisations. Seen from this perspective 'smuggling' becomes a broader category that can include privileged authorities that hold power and make decisions regarding the prolonged liminal life and death experienced by the displaced and exiled.[11] In fact, actors given the responsibility of care and oversight are often guilty of causing the greatest misery and obstacles to safety and freedom.[12]

What distinguishes the politicised and sensational discourse on people smugglers from more nuanced critical readings is the attention to the different forms of smuggling, the practices of those who organise smuggling, and fluidity and unpredictable nature of border crossing endeavours. Border control discourse tends to treat people smuggling as an issue that can be defined with one basic account or something one dimensional. In reality there are many different forms, many different practices, and many different combinations and configurations of forms and practices. There are smugglers who are noble while others are horrible, some others are slightly worrying while others are very problematic, and there are myriad motivations driving all these examples. Clearly, there is no singular account.

Border crossing through the use of smugglers is a transgressive act on numerous levels and helps expose many of the social, cultural, economic and political problems associated with modern global human movement. Attempts by states to stop global human movement by eradicating people smuggling has only transformed the practice by redirected travel routes and in many cases made the journeys more dangerous. Smugglers have responded by rearranging their transnational networks and tactics in order to identify new opportunities and strategies. Harsh laws introduced by states aiming to end people smuggling have failed and as a result people seeking safety and protection are now facing increasingly more difficult and hazardous pathways to freedom.[13] One can only justify the combination of criminalisation and demonisation of people smugglers if first the impacts of state laws and policies are ignored altogether. Also, such attempts at justification must ignore the insights and analyses of those with lived experiences of being smuggled. The justification of border violence which drives people to risk their lives embarking on dangerous voyages becomes impossible when more complex perspectives are considered and critically understood. The public debate about people smugglers as it stands is a long way from acknowledging that some practitioners may also have humanitarian intentions or political visions that challenge border violence enacted or facilitated by states and the international community.

Over the years of working with people who had lost family members in boat disasters I heard stories of how smugglers lied about the type of boat, the condition of the boat and nature of the journey. Other people seeking protection described how smugglers sent their own family members to safety, made exceptions for people who could not afford the whole fee or waived the fee entirely. Refugees have explained how smugglers expressed concern and made special preparations for women, children or sick people. However, others described various forms of discrimination

based on gender and race, and also examples of abuse
and theft.

In a conversation with a people smuggler in Iran I
noticed how he took pride in his work and saw it as a form
of resistance against a state that oppressed its citizens and the
people living along its borders. The smuggler made clear to
me that he was both a Kurd and a Sunni, indicating that his
status as a marginalised person provided him with a special
understanding of politics and society in Iran.[14] For him,
engaging in people smuggling was a noble act and a way of
challenging state violence – he was so assured of his position
that he shared it to me in a public place with passers-by
listening to our discussion. He drew strength from the unique
combination of his ethnic, religious and political identities
and his practices, and he interpreted his role in society as
potential for positive transformation.[15]

In the face of border violence people smuggling can also
be directly or indirectly interpreted as a radical disruption
of discriminatory practices. Facilitating peoples' border
crossing in this way becomes a form of activism for universal
travel equity by usurping the state's monopoly on forms and
methods of human movement and the discriminatory limits
pertaining to access and opportunity. People smuggling
unsettles the social imaginary related to borders, forces us to
rethink the positionalities of those who are not represented
in visions of justice, and questions the sanctity dangerously
associated with passports and visas. As a technology
of power, people smuggling can be both liberating and
exploitative, and many other things in conjunction. It
challenges the language we use in relation to citizenship and
our views regarding order, responsibility and fairness. People
smuggling is transgressive because in some cases it can be

both a humanitarian act and a crime, and so much more. It is a practice in which people have been thrown together by violent and powerful global forces,[16] an ambiguous and fluid practice that generates new forms of competition, negotiation and resolution.

BEHROUZ BOOCHANI:

The debate regarding people smugglers must be understood by focusing on the process of migration or seeking asylum. From its beginning to end it involves someone moving from their place of origin to a new destination and pertains to the relationship between two sides: the smuggler and the person seeking asylum. These two parties characterise the situation. It is significant to note that in relation to the public image of the people smuggler, what we know from the media and according to politicians or the official accounts, the voices of smugglers and people seeking asylum are suppressed.[17] It is rare to ask the opinions of a smuggler and request that they describe this practice, it is rare to ask a refugee to describe the process. Whatever the situation, smuggling is not a cruel criminal offence. The account provided by governments and the mainstream media is a form of criminalisation – when they speak about smugglers they describe their actions as a great crime, they are described as terrible criminals. However, when one asks smugglers and people seeking asylum they present perspectives that conflict with the criminalisation discourse. They do not reduce smuggling to a crime. They feel very different about it – this is really important. Considering the views of these two actors is a form of decriminalising.

The very notion of a people smuggler needs further analysis. The name smuggler is given to the person who finds clients and it is also used for the person who is a level above the person who presents the customers. That person then introduces them to someone even higher up. In reality, what we are faced with is multiple roles, different roles that are all labelled as people smugglers. But there is a big difference in the profit that each one makes and the work they do. To help explain what goes on let me elaborate on the system in Indonesia. Now just imagine there is a person in Afghanistan who needs to get to Australia, this person is first introduced to someone and after some conversation they agree on, say, $5000 to help them travel to Australia. The person who is the smuggler in Afghanistan or Iran is working with a series of smugglers in Indonesia and their role is to find clients. The person fleeing only knows that first point of contact – the one they give the money to. The responsibility rests solely on that person. The money changes hands and a promise is made to send that person – there is one point of contact who is connected to a wider network. In reality, that first person just introduces the client to another smuggler, and so the smuggler that is one level up accumulates groups of various numbers from different smugglers. They then manage these groups and interact with someone working above them. There are many different relationships taking place here. This then reaches the most senior smuggler, someone who arranges the boat going to Australia. That person probably has an extremely high rank in the police or maybe they are a politician in the parliament, or even a major political actor of another kind – all these kinds of people are involved in people smuggling. All the people described in this process are labelled people smugglers even though they have very different roles. The person seeking asylum will never come face to face with the most senior smuggler who manages this chain. Even the smugglers that interact with the person fleeing do not interact with the head smuggler – they only ever deal with the people in the middle.

What a person seeking asylum is faced with is smugglers of different rank, incomes of various range, with different levels of power. We are faced with a system of differing scales, even though everyone is described as a smuggler. There are smugglers who are at the bottom of the pecking order and those who are at the head of the network and then even more powerful ones. This is a trade that involves billions of dollars and the money goes to many different people. The one at the bottom gets the least and it gradually goes up. In the middle there are people who are not engaged in smuggling but facilitate the smuggling practices. For example, there may be a police commander who the head smuggler works with. They get a bribe and they allow people to board and pass through on a particular day. They are not smuggling directly, but one can say indirectly.

The smugglers who are part of this process have different motivations. Without a doubt money and the establishment of a business are the fundamental factors. You will not find anyone who will say they are doing it just to save people. There are people who are also motivated by helping people but when they are arrested, they are charged with people smuggling even though at some point they just wanted to help someone cross borders to safety. But, in general, the people involved in this are looking to do business and make money. Alongside this they may also have other motivations, and this depends on individuals. Some only want to do business, some feel like they are engaging in a political act, some feel they are helping people, although they make money, they feel it is their right to earn an income. The variables are great, we cannot offer a single description for a people smuggler since everyone has a range of different motivations – even though business is the most dominant. There are some for whom the life of human beings has little worth and others who make human life the priority. Some smugglers work with integrity and are committed to their promise to ensure people arrive safely. Different motivations, different roles, and different kinds of behaviour. There is no one category that covers all of these, we cannot just say they are simply good or bad.

Over the last six years the policy of the Australian Government has been to turn back boats that arrive in Australian waters.[18] In some cases, they would repair them, sometimes they would give the passengers food and water, and then without letting them leave the boat they would turn them around and push them back to the open seas. It is significant that there has been no study done on the future of these people who were turned back. Did these people survive? What happened after they were turned back? This whole policy was done under the veil of secrecy. This is exactly what people smugglers do. The nature of a smuggler's work is to complete the process in secret. Australia has effectively been doing the same with its boat turn back policy, when exiling people to Manus and Nauru, and when transferring people from Manus and Nauru to Australia.[19] These acts have never been announced in the media and are always done under a shroud of secrecy.[20]

If we ask refugees what they think of people smugglers they will respond based on their own personal experiences. The description by someone who was successful in their journey and arrived safely will offer a positive account, but someone whose money was stolen or who lost family members will respond negatively and demand the smugglers be arrested and tried. The experience will determine the different impressions.

Conclusion

In conclusion, we, the co-authors, return to where we began in stressing the key role of the state in creating the myths of the people smuggler as the solitary evil figure in the lives of asylum seekers taking boat journeys in search of protection. In contrast, we seek to highlight that the state, in this case Australia, is deeply implicated in the interconnected hardships, deprivations and rights abuses asylum seekers face. Turning the people smuggler into the primary figure of focus and derision, mitigates and hides the key responsibility states have in ensuring the fundamental right to claim protection from persecution, a right that has to be accompanied with freedom of movement. We end with an extract from *No Friend but the Mountains*, where Behrouz recalls the intense emotions of his own boat journey to Australia:

> Two trucks carry scared and restless passengers down a winding, rocky labyrinth. They speed along a road surrounded by jungle, the exhaust emitting frightening roars. Black cloth is wrapped around the vehicles, so we can only see the stars above. Women and men sit beside each other, their children on their laps ... we look up at the sky the colour of intense anxiety. Every so often someone slightly adjusts their position on the truck's wooden floor to allow the blood to circulate through tired muscles. Worn out from sitting, we still need to conserve our strength to cope with the rest of the journey ... In the three months I was in Jakarta's Kalibata City and on Kendari Island, I would regularly

hear news of boats that had sunk. But one always thinks that such fatal incidents only befall others – it's hard to believe you may face death.

One imagines one's own death differently to the death of others. I can't imagine it. Could it be that these trucks travelling in convoy, rushing towards the ocean, are couriers of death?[21]

Translation of Behrouz's contribution by Omid Tofighian

NOTES

Introduction: People smuggling and Australian migration history

1   Emma Rodgers, 'Rudd wants people smugglers to "rot in hell"', *ABC News*, 17 April 2009, <www.abc.net.au/news/2009-04-17/rudd-wants-people-smugglers-to-rot-in-hell/1653814>. Accessed 5 August 2020.

2   Mario Kaiser, 'The People Smugglers', *Transition*, 90 (2001), 39.

3   Libby Garland, *After They Closed the Gates: Jewish Illegal Immigration to the United States, 1921–1965* (Chicago: University of Chicago Press, 2014), p. 3.

4   Garland, *After They Closed the Gates*, p. 154.

5   Leanne Weber and Sharon Pickering use the term 'illegalized travellers'. Leanne Weber and Sharon Pickering, *Globalization and Borders: Death at the Global Frontier* (Basingstoke: Palgrave Macmillan, 2011).

6   Tony Kevin, *Reluctant Rescuers* (Canberra: Self-published, 2012).

7   Robin de Crespigny, *The People Smuggler: The True Story of Ali Al Jenabi* (Melbourne: Penguin Books, 2012).

8   Dawood Amiri, *Confessions of a People Smuggler* (Melbourne: Scribe, 2014), pp. 16–17.

9   Kaiser, 'The People Smugglers', 30–41, 35.

10 Kaiser, 'The People Smugglers', 33.

11 UNODC, *Global Study on Smuggling of Migrants*, 2018, United Nations publication, Sales No. E.18.IV.9, 2018, p. 5, <https://www.unodc.org/documents/data-and-analysis/glosom/GLOSOM_2018_web_small.pdf>. Accessed 10 November 2019.

12 Anh Do, *The Happiest Refugee* (Crows Nest: Allen and Unwin, 2010), p. 9.

13 Amiri, *Confessions of a People Smuggler*, p. 178.

14 Marie McAuliffe and Khalid Koser, eds, *A Long Way to Go: Irregular Migration Patterns, Processes, Drivers and Decision-Making* (Canberra, ANU Press, 2017), p.35, <https://press-files.anu.edu.au/downloads/press/n4016/pdf/book.pdf>. Accessed 10 March 2021.

15 Gadi Benezer and Roger Zetter, 'Searching for Directions: Conceptual and Methodological Challenges in Researching Refugee Journeys', *Journal of Refugee Studies*, 28:3 (2014), 297–318, 299.

1   Escaping the Holocaust by breaking the law: Courage and disobedience

1   Masha Frydman, Interview 26576, Segment 18, *Visual History Archive*, USC Shoah Foundation, 1999.

2   Frydman, Interview 26576, Segment 25.

3   Frydman, Interview 26576, Segment 26.

4   Masha Zeleznikow, Interview 26576, Segment 130, *Visual History Archive*, USC Shoah Foundation, 1999.

5   Leopold Zylberman, Interview 27150, Segment 130. *Visual History Archive*, USC Shoah Foundation, 1999.

6   Helen Granek, Interview 21527, Segments 12, 22. *Visual History Archive*, USC Shoah Foundation, 1999.
7   When the consulate was closed and Sugihara transferred, he continued to issue visas, from German-occupied Prague, and then from Königsberg. On his return to Japan in 1947, Sugihara was ordered to resign from the Foreign Service. He held a number of different jobs, and died in 1986.
8   Hillel Levine, *In Search of Sugihara: The Elusive Japanese Diplomat Who Risked his Life to Rescue 10,000 Jews from the Holocaust* (New York: The Free Press, 1996), p. 125.
9   Stephen Muller, Interview 4764, Segment 41. *Visual History Archive*, USC Shoah Foundation, 1999.
10   Christopher Heathcote, 'Mora, Georges (1913–1992)', *Australian Dictionary of Biography*, Australian National University, <www.adb.anu.edu.au/biography/mora-georges-23840>. Accessed 3 July 2018.
11   Philippe Mora, *Monsieur Mayonnaise*, Yarra Bank Films, 2016; Antidote Films, 2017. Written, produced and directed by Trevor Graham.
12   Lola Snow, Interview 5740, Segment 59. *Visual History Archive*, USC Shoah Foundation, 1999.
13   See the discussion in the Introduction to *Shelter from the Holocaust: Rethinking Jewish Survival in the Soviet Union*, Mark Edele, Sheila Fitzpatrick and Atina Grossman, eds (Detroit: Wayne State University Press, 2017).
14   Wislawa Szymborska, 'Could Have', in *View with a Grain of Sand: Selected Poems*, trans. Stanislaw Barańczak and Clare Cavanagh (New York: Harcourt Brace and Company, 1996), pp. 65–66, cited in Clendinnen, *Reading the Holocaust* (Melbourne: Text Publishing, 1998), p. 207.

2   A Jewish refugee racket
1   'Jewish Landing Permit Holders', Memo for the Secretary, Department of Immigration, no date. NAA: 9306, 355/3.
2   For a discussion of this, see Klaus Neumann, *Across the Seas: Australia's Responses to Refugees* (Collingwood: Black Inc, 2015), pp. 85–96.
3   'Black-Market Racket in Aust. Migrants', *Daily Telegraph*, 20 January 1949, 1.
4   'Major Migrant Racket', *Brisbane Telegraph*, 19 October 1949, 1.
5   Henry Gullett statement in House of Representatives, November 27, 1946, *Commonwealth Parliamentary Debates*, Representatives, Vol. 189, 661.
6   Suzanne Rutland and Sol Encel, 'No Room at the Inn: American Responses to Australian Immigration Policies, 1946–54', *Patterns of Prejudice*, 43:5 (2009), 497–518, 501.
7   Interview with Harold Grant, Related Material, Film Australia *Immigration* DVD, 195 mins, 2004.
8   Form 40, in operation before the war, included the question, 'Are you Jewish?' The consensus among historians nowadays is that this question was designed as a bureaucratic means of enforcing anti-Semitic immigration restrictions. Suzanne Rutland, '"Are you Jewish?" Postwar Jewish Immigration to Australia, 1945–1954', *Australian Journal of Jewish Studies*, V:2 (1991), 35–58; Paul Bartrop, 'The "Jewish Race Clause" in Australian Immigration Forms', *Australian Jewish Historical Society Journal*, 11:1 (1990), 69–78.
9   David Horner, *The Spy Catchers: The Official History of ASIO, 1949–1963* (Crows Nest: Allen and Unwin, 2014), p. 251.
10   'Report from K Turbayne to Chief Migration Officer, on Landing Permits – Austria, dated 16 February 1950', NAA: A9306, 355/3.

11   'Landing Permits Austria', memo to the Chief Migration Officer, 17 May 1950, NAA:
      A9306, 355/3.

12   NAA: A9306, 355/3.

13   Frederick Wurbell and Thurston Clarke put the number of Jewish partisans under
      Teicholz's leadership at 300. Frederick E Wurbell and Thurston Clarke, *Lost Hero: The
      Mystery of Raoul Wallenberg* (New York: McGraw Hill Book Company, 1982), p. 52.

14   Wurbell and Clarke, *Lost Hero*, p. 52.

15   Wurbell and Clarke, *Lost Hero*, pp. 53–54.

16   Teicholz's biography is taken from a number of sources. See the description by his son
      Tom Teicholz in *Encyclopaedia Judaica* and *Jewish Journal*; and Yehuda Bauer, *Flight and
      Rescue: Brichah* (New York, Random House, 1970), pp. 158–62. On the Rothschild
      Spital, see Ada Schein, 'Health Care Services for Holocaust Survivors in Postwar
      Austria, 1945–1952: A Pattern of Jewish Solidarity', in Francoise S Ouzan and Manfred
      Gerstenfeld, eds, *Postwar Jewish Displacement and Rebirth 1945–1953* (Leiden and
      Boston, Brill, 2014), pp. 46–59.

17   Mark Aarons, *Sanctuary: Nazi Fugitives in Australia* (Port Melbourne, William
      Heinemann, 1989), p. 11.

18   Memo no. 49/3/77, Department of Immigration. NAA: A445, 235/1/24. My thanks to
      Suzanne Rutland for alerting me to this document.

19   Libby Garland, *After They Closed the Gates: Jewish Illegal Immigration to the United
      States, 1921–1965* (Chicago, University of Chicago Press, 2014), p. 131.

20   Joseph Roth, *The Wandering Jews*, trans. Michael Hoffman (New York and London,
      WW Norton and Company, 2001), p. 59.

21   Figures given by WD Rubinstein, *Jews In Australia*, p. 67. Quote from 'New Policy for
      Enemy Aliens', NAA: A445, 235/1/24.

22   Report from WK McCoy to the Chief Migration Officer on Australian Landing Permit
      Procedure in Vienna, 17 January 1952', NAA: A9306, 355/1.

23   Quoted in Tara Zahra, '"Prisoners of the Postwar": Expellees, Displaced Persons and
      Jews in Austria after World War II', *Austrian History Yearbook*, 41 (2010), 205.

24   WD Rubenstein, *The Jews in Australia: A Thematic History. Volume Two, 1945 to the
      Present* (Melbourne, William Heinemann, 1991), p. 52.

3   Les Murray: We would have had a beer

1   Les Murray, *By the Balls: Memoir of a Football Tragic* (Sydney: Random House, 2006).

2   Murray, *By the Balls*, pp. 20–21.

3   Murray, *By the Balls*, p. 21.

4   Murray, *By the Balls*, pp. 23–24.

5   Murray, *By the Balls*, p. 25.

6   Murray, *By the Balls*, pp. 26–27.

7   Murray, *By the Balls*, p. 28.

8   Murray, *By the Balls*, p. 45.

9   'Les Murray's Mission', *Dateline*, Episode 36, 2011, <www.sbs.com.au/ondemand/
      video/11790403964/dateline-les-murrays-missionvoting-for-freedom>. Accessed
      25 March 2020.

10   TISM, 'What Nationality is Les Murray?', *Machiavelli and the Four Seasons*, Studio
      Album (London and Los Angeles: Shock Records, 1995).

4   Silvie Luscombe: Connections

1   Information about Maribyrnong Migrant Hostel was drawn from Pamie Ching Tsz
      Fung, 'A Place "Midway" Between the Old Life and the New: A Case Study of the
      Migrant Hostel at Maribyrnong', PhD dissertation, University of Melbourne, 2013.

5   **Phung: A leaf in the ocean**
     Nathalie Huynh Chau Nguyen is an Associate Professor of History at Monash
     University. An Oxford graduate and award-winning researcher, she is a leading scholar
     of the Vietnamese diaspora and the author of four books including *Voyage of Hope:
     Vietnamese Australian Women's Narratives* (2005), *Memory Is Another Country: Women
     of the Vietnamese Diaspora* (2009) and *South Vietnamese Soldiers: Memories of the
     Vietnam War and After* (2016)

1   See Keith St Cartmail, *Exodus Indochina* (Auckland: Heinemann, 1983), pp. 8, 12,
     227; Linda Hitchcox, *Vietnamese Refugees in Southeast Asian Camps* (Basingstoke:
     Macmillan in association with St Antony's College, Oxford, 1990), p. 85; W Courtland
     Robinson, *Terms of Refuge: The Indochinese Exodus and the International Response*
     (London: Zed Books, 1998), p. 59; Mary Terrell Cargill and Jade Quang Huynh,
     Voices of Vietnamese Boat People: Nineteen Narratives of Escape and Survival (Jefferson:
     McFarland, 2000), p. 4.

2   For conditions in post-war Vietnam, see United Nations High Commissioner for
     Refugees, *The State of the World's Refugees: Fifty Years of Humanitarian Action* (Oxford:
     Oxford University Press, 2000), p. 82; Jacqueline Desbarats, 'Human Rights: Two
     Steps Forward, One Step Back?', in *Vietnam Today: Assessing the New Trends*, Thai
     Quang Trung, ed. (New York: Crane Russak, 1990), pp. 47–64; Hitchcox, *Vietnamese
     Refugees*, pp. 37–68; James M Freeman and Nguyen Dinh Huu, *Voices from the Camps:
     Vietnamese Children Seeking Asylum* (Seattle: University of Washington Press, 2003),
     p. 7; Steven DeBonis, *Children of the Enemy: Oral Histories of Vietnamese Amerasians
     and Their Mothers* (Jefferson: McFarland, 1995); Robert S McKelvey, *The Dust of Life:
     America's Children Abandoned in Vietnam* (Seattle: University of Washington Press,
     1999).

3   Robinson, *Terms of Refuge*, p. 28; St Cartmail, *Exodus Indochina*, p. 99.

4   St Cartmail, *Exodus Indochina*, p. 101.

5   Quoted in Robinson, *Terms of Refuge*, p. 40.

6   St Cartmail, *Exodus Indochina*, p. 26.

7   Robinson, *Terms of Refuge*, p. 52. See also St Cartmail, *Exodus Indochina*, p. 101.

8   Robinson, *Terms of Refuge*, pp. 179–80.

9   See Kien Nguyen, *The Unwanted* (Sydney: Pan Macmillan, 2001), p. 245.

10   See Nathalie Huynh Chau Nguyen, *Voyage of Hope: Vietnamese Australian Women's
     Narratives* (Altona: Common Ground Publishing, 2005), p. 16.

11   St Cartmail, *Exodus Indochina*, p. 9.

12   See Australian Bureau of Statistics, 2016 Census Media Release: Census reveals a fast
     changing, *culturally diverse nation*, 27 June 2017, <www.abs.gov.au/AUSSTATS/abs@.
     nsf/mediareleasesbyReleaseDate/BA4418859C270D68CA2581BF001E65B3>.
     Accessed 5 August 2020; Christine McMurray, *Community Profiles 1996 Census: Viet
     Nam Born* (Belconnen: Department of Immigration and Multicultural Affairs, 1999);
     Nancy Viviani, *The Indochinese in Australia 1975–1995: From Burnt Boats to Barbecues*
     (Melbourne: Oxford University Press, 1996), p. 1; Mandy Thomas, 'The Vietnamese
     in Australia,' in *Asians in Australia: Patterns of Migration and Settlement,* James E
     Coughlan and Deborah J McNamara, eds (Melbourne: Macmillan Education, 1997),
     pp. 274–95; and *Country Profile: Vietnam*, Australian Government Department of
     Immigration and Border Protection, 2016.

6   **Carina Hoang: My people smuggler was my saviour**

1   For more on this history, see United Nations High Commissioner for Refugees,
     'Chapter 4: Flight from Indochina', *The State of the World's Refugees: Fifty Years of*

Humanitarian Action, 1 January 2000, <www.unhcr.org/3ebf9bad0.html>. Accessed 31 August 2020.

2   UNICEF, 'Child Displacement', April 2020: <data.unicef.org/topic/child-migration-and-displacement/displacement/>. Accessed 15 February 2020.

7   From the horse's mouth

Phuong Ngo is a Vietnamese-Australian artist and curator living and working in Naarm (Melbourne). He is currently co-director of Hyphenated Projects with Nikki Lam, and curator at large at the Substation. His practice is concerned with the interpretation of history, memory and place, and how it impacts individual and collective identity of the Vietnamese diaspora.

9   Munjed Al Muderis: A journey of many legs

1   Munjed Al Muderis and Patrick Weaver, *Walking Free* (Crows Nest: Allen and Unwin, 2015), pp. 134–35.

10   Taozen: Entrepreneur

1   Amin Saikal, *Modern Afghanistan: A History of Struggle and Survival* (New York: Palgrave Macmillan, 2004), p. 1.

11   Lena Hattom: Coming to Australia on the *SIEV-IV*. One family's journey

1   Mandaean Human Rights Group, *Mandaean Human Rights Annual Report*, March 2008, p. 6.

2   STAARTS, *Mandaean Community Consultation Report*, 29 October 2006 (revised September 2008), p. 17.

3   United States Committee for Refugees and Immigrants, *US Committee for Refugees World Refugee Survey 2000 – Jordan*, 1 June 2000, available at <www.refworld.org/docid/3ae6a8d220.html>. Accessed 9 March 2020.

4   David Marr and Marian Wilkinson, *Dark Victory* (Crows Nest: Allen and Unwin, 2003), p. 242.

12   Aye Min Soe: Shooting soldiers

1   The name of Burma was changed to Myanmar in 1989 by the ruling junta. Aye Min uses the two names interchangeably. I have referred to Burma pre-1989 and Myanmar after that date.

2   Benedict Rogers, 'Burma's ruler: brutal, reclusive, and a skilled manipulator', *The Independent*, 3 August 2009 <www.independent.co.uk/news/world/asia/burmas-ruler-brutal-reclusive-ndash-and-a-skilled-manipulator-1766568>. Accessed 24 September 2019.

3   John Anderson, 'Monks, tanks and videotape', *New York Times*, 15 May 2009 <www.archive.nytimes.com/www.nytimes.com/2009/05/17/movies/17ande>. Accessed 24 September 2019.

4   'Response to cyclone in Myanmar "unacceptably slow" – Ban Ki-moon', UN News, 12 May 2008 <www.news.un.org/en/story/2008/05/259002-response-cyclone-myanmar-unacceptably-slow-ban-ki-moon>. Accessed 24 September 2019.

13   The multiple faces of the people smuggler

Behrouz Boochani is Adjunct Associate Professor of Social Sciences at UNSW, author and journalist. His book *No Friend but the Mountains: Writing From Manus Prison* (Picador 2018) has won numerous awards including the 2019 Victorian Prize for Literature.

Claudia Tazreiter is Associate Professor of Sociology at UNSW. She is co-convenor of the Forced Migration Research Network.

Omid Tofighian is an award-winning lecturer, researcher and community advocate affiliated with Birkbeck, University of London, and University of Sydney. His translation of Behrouz Boochani's book *No Friend but the Mountains: Writing From Manus Prison* (Picador 2018) has won numerous awards including the 2019 Victorian Prize for Literature.

1   Sharon Pickering, Claudia Tazreiter, Rebecca Powell and James Barry, 'Information consumption and decision making of irregular migrants in Indonesia', Research Programme, Occasional Paper Series, Department of Immigration and Border Protection, Australian Government, no. 19 (2016), pp. 1–43; Claudia Tazreiter, Sharon Pickering and Rebecca Powell, 'Rohingya Women in Malaysia: Decision-making and Information Sharing in the Course of Irregular Migration', Robert Schuman Centre for Advanced Studies, RSCAS 2017/55, Global Governance Programme-283, *EUI Working Paper Series*, European University Institute (2017), pp 1–42.

2   Nandita Rani Sharma, *Home Rule. National Sovereignty and the Separation of Natives and Migrants* (Durham & London: Duke University Press, 2020).

3   Claudia Tazreiter, *Asylum Seekers and the State: The Politics of Protection in a Security-Conscious World* (Aldershot: Ashgate, 2004); Claudia Tazreiter, 'Lifeboat Politics in the Pacific: Affect and the Ripples and Shimmers of a Migrant Saturated Future', *Emotion, Space and Society*, 16 (2015), 99–107; Claudia Tazreiter, 'The Unlucky in the "Lucky Country": Asylum Seekers, Irregular Migrants and Refugees and Australia's Politics of Disappearance', *Australian Journal of Human Rights*, 23:2 (2017), 242–60.

4   Marilyn Lake and Henry Reynolds, *Colour Bar. The International Challenge of Racial Equality* (Cambridge: Cambridge University Press, 2008).

5   Catriona Elder, *Being Australian. Narratives of National Identity* (Crows Nest: Allen and Unwin, 2007), p. 10.

6   Sandro Mezzadra and Brett Neilson, *Border as Method, or, the Multiplication of Labor* (Durham: Duke University Press, 2013).

7   Marc Augé, *Non-Places: Introduction to an Anthropology of Supermodernity*, trans. J Howe (London: Verso, 1992).

8   Claudia Tazreiter, 'The Unlucky in the "Lucky Country": Asylum Seekers, Irregular Migrants and Refugees and Australia's Politics of Disappearance', *Australian Journal of Human Rights*, 23:2 (2017), 242–60.

9   Omid Tofighian, 'Debordering Academia: Centring the Displaced and Exiled in Research. Foreword', *Alphaville: Journal of Film and Screen Media*, 18 (2019), 1–2.

10 Omid Tofighian, 'Introducing Manus Prison Theory: Knowing Border Violence', *Globalizations*, 17:7 (2020), 1138–1156.

11 Behrouz Boochani, 'Manus Police Pulled My Hair and Beat Me. "You've Damaged Our Reputation," They Said,' trans. O Tofighian, *The Guardian*, 24 November 2017, <www.theguardian.com/australia-news/commentisfree/2017/nov/24/manus-police-pulled-my-hair-and-beat-me-youve-damaged-our-reputation-they-said>. Accessed 5 August 2020.

12 Behrouz Boochani, 'How Many More People Must Die on Manus Before Australia Ends Indefinite Detention', trans. O Tofighian, *The Guardian*, 3 June 2019, <www.theguardian.com/commentisfree/2019/jun/03/how-many-more-people-must-die-on-manus-before-australia-ends-indefinite-detention>. Accessed 5 August 2020; Erfan Dana, 'Erfan Dana', trans. O Tofighian, Writing Through Fences, 2018 <www.writingthroughfences.org/writers/erfan-dana/>. Accessed 5 August 2020; Omid

Tofighian, 'Black Bodies for Political Profit: Sudanese and Somali Standpoints on Australia's Racialised Border Regime', *Transition*, 126 (2018), 5–18.

13   Behrouz Boochani and Omid Tofighian, 'The Last Days in Manus Prison', *Meanjin* (Summer 2018) <www.meanjin.com.au/essays/the-last-days-in-manus-prison>. Accessed 5 August 2020; Behrouz Boochani, '"The Boats are Coming" is One of the Greatest Lies Told to the Australian People', trans. O Tofighian, *The Guardian*, 1 July 2019, <www.theguardian.com/commentisfree/2019/jul/02/the-boats-are-coming-is-one-of-the-greatest-lies-told-to-the-australian-people>. Accessed 5 August 2020; Jeremy Elphick, 'Cinematic Poetics and Reclaiming History: "Chauka, Please Tell Us the Time" as Legacy', (trans. of interviews O Tofighian), *Alphaville: Journal of Film and Screen Media*, 18 (2019), 199–204.

14   Omid Tofighian, 'Sanctions, Refugees and the Marginalised: Iran Uprisings Are Australia's Concern Too', *ABC News*, 6 January 2018, <www.abc.net.au/news/2018-01-06/iran-uprising-australia-manus-island-political-refugees-islamic/9305756>. Accessed 5 August 2020.

15   For a similar discussion of positionality and epistemology, see Omid Tofighian, 'Behrouz Boochani and the Manus Prison Narratives: Merging Translation with Philosophical Reading', *Continuum: Journal of Media and Cultural Studies*, 32:4 (2018), 1–9.

16   B Boochani, D Flores, A Sibanda, V Mujakachi, Temboman*, Fafa*, R Huzzard, L Cape-Davenhill, A Sirriyeh, H Lewis, G Lonergan, D Conlon, B Bennett and O Tofighian, 'Transnational Communities for Dismantling Detention: From Manus Island to the UK', *Community Psychology in Global Perspective*, 6:1 (2020), 108–28.

17   Omid Tofighian, 'Disregard, Dismissal and Divestment: Behrouz Boochani, Academia and the Media', PEN International, 20 June 2019, <www.pen-international.org/news/disregard-dismissal-and-divestment-behrouz-boochani-academia-and-the-media>. Accessed 5 August 2020.

18   Behrouz Boochani, '"The Boats are Coming" is One of the Greatest Lies Told to the Australian People', trans. O Tofighian, *The Guardian*, 1 July 2019, <www.theguardian.com/commentisfree/2019/jul/02/the-boats-are-coming-is-one-of-the-greatest-lies-told-to-the-australian-people>. Accessed 5 August 2020.

19   Behrouz Boochani, 'Exile', trans. O Tofighian, *Art + Australia*, 5 (August 2019).

20   Behrouz Boochani, 'I Write From Manus as a Duty to History', trans. O Tofighian, *The Guardian*, 6 December 2017, <www.theguardian.com/commentisfree/2017/dec/06/i-write-from-manus-island-as-a-duty-to-history>. Accessed 5 August 2020; Behrouz Boochani, '"This is Hell Out Here". How Behrouz Boochani's Diaries Expose Australia's Refugee Shame', trans. O Tofighian, *The Guardian*, 4 December 2017, <www.theguardian.com/world/2017/dec/04/this-is-hell-behrouz-boochani-diaries-expose-australia-refugee-shame>. Accessed 5 August 2020; Behrouz Boochani, 'All We Want is Freedom – Not Another Prison Camp', trans. O Tofighian, *The Guardian*, 13 November 2017, <www.theguardian.com/commentisfree/2017/nov/13/all-we-want-is-freedom-not-another-prison-camp>. Accessed 5 August 2020.

21   Behrouz Boochani, *No Friend but the Mountains: Writing From Manus Prison*, trans. O Tofighian (Sydney: Picador/Pan Macmillan, 2018), pp. 1–3.

ACKNOWLEDGMENTS

This book could not have been written without the many contributors who so generously shared their stories. We were enriched and humbled by the time we spent with them. We were introduced to several of our contributors by Bwe Thay, himself a refugee, and who has worked tirelessly as a refugee advocate since he came to Australia. We owe him grateful thanks, as we do the wonderful Phillipa McGuinness, who, while still at NewSouth Publishing, saw the potential in this book. Our thanks to Paul O'Beirne, Joumana Awad and Elspeth Menzies who have shepherded us through the publishing process with such grace. A special thank you to our wonderful copy editor, Briony Neilson.

This book is a true collaboration. It is a project of which we are both enormously proud, and we are happy to have had the chance to work together to bring to light a work that speaks personally and strongly to each of us. We dedicate it to the memory of our respective grandparents; Julie's grandmother Shaindl, and Ruth's grandfather Sándor Grozinger, whose defiance of hostile laws allowed them and their descendants, not only to survive, but to thrive.

INDEX